THE BELIEVERS GUIDE TO BUILDING WEALTH

THE BELIEVERS GUIDE TO BUILDING WEALTH

A Guide to Financial Independence, Wealth, Debt-Free Living, and Estate Planning

WILLIAM L. NEILL

Copyright © 2016 by William L. Neill.

Library of Congress Control Number: 2016909103
ISBN: Hardcover 978-1-5245-0754-1
　　　 Softcover 978-1-5245-0753-4
　　　 eBook 978-1-5245-0752-7

All rights reserved. No part of this book may be reproduced or transmitted in any form or by any means, electronic or mechanical, including photocopying, recording, or by any information storage and retrieval system, without permission in writing from the copyright owner.

This is a work of fiction. Names, characters, places and incidents either are the product of the author's imagination or are used fictitiously, and any resemblance to any actual persons, living or dead, events, or locales is entirely coincidental.

Any people depicted in stock imagery provided by Thinkstock are models, and such images are being used for illustrative purposes only.
Certain stock imagery © Thinkstock.

Print information available on the last page.

Rev. date: 06/10/2016

To order additional copies of this book, contact:
Xlibris
1-888-795-4274
www.Xlibris.com
Orders@Xlibris.com
741867

CONTENTS

Preface vii
Introduction ix
Chapter 1   A Spiritual Foundation 1
Chapter 2   Dispelling the Myths 5
Chapter 3   What is Money? 9
Chapter 4   Asset Management 13
Chapter 5   Putting a Plan Together 22
Chapter 6   Understanding Investing 35
Chapter 7   Compound Interest, the Rule of 72 and Risk 41
Chapter 8   Credit and Debt Elimination 48
Chapter 9   Creating Income Producing Ventures 53
Chapter 10 Estate Planning and End of Life Care 57
Chapter 11 Acknowledgments and References 61
Chapter 12 Appendix 64

PREFACE

I was encouraged to produce this work because of my previous background in marketing and the financial services arena. I really enjoyed the opportunity to meet folk, and have the ability to change their financial future forever by sharing with them simple principles of money, debt elimination, and wealth building. It's a good feeling when you introduce yourself and what you do for folk, and a professional relationship of trust begins and continues for a life time. When you can simply make an assessment of how they are doing things financially, and proposed to them how using the same funds they spend monthly would change into greater benefit for them and their family just by repositioning how they are doing business now. I've had that experience to deliver to a mother with two high school teenagers a check from the death of her husband. The difference in what they were doing and what they decided to do after we worked with them, and presented them with all the relevant facts was absolutely amazing. Instead of receiving a death benefit check for the $40,000 to carry them on in life, they were given a check for $150,000. Still much lower than where they should have been, but at least two and a half times more than what was in place. This is what this book is all about, and why I want the blessed privilege to share with you, the reader, how you can take advantage of benefits financially available to you by simply repositioning what you are doing to increase those benefits. I will share with you principles that make sense, but have not really been presented to the audience I am writing to now. The principles I will share with you have been around for ages. Unfortunately, they were for a privileged few. I am also excited about working with a team of folk who feel like I do, and are also on a crusade to change the financial conditions in families, particularly who are saved and labor in the kingdom of God! You will learn the principle of the decreasing responsibility theory; building an alternative credit file to offset the erroneous one you have, or if you had problems with credit, how to get back; building wealth and an estate while serving in the kingdom of God, and how to protect those assets in the event of unexpected trauma; the rule of seventy-two (72), how to understand compounding your interest to grow your savings and investments; advanced directives (a living will) and a general will; and my big one, eliminating debt.

It will be so simple, you will be amazed at little mistakes you make. I will teach you step-by-step. If you will give yourself time, and make a commitment to improve your total financial mindset and practice, you will see a change in ninety days! That's right, if you follow the instructions in this book, step-by-step, you will realize a change within the first week of reading this work. You must know I want you to *win*! My good friend who encouraged me to do this work admonished me that God did not give this knowledge to me just for my own benefit, but to develop kingdom partners in this area. I have a cousin in Georgia who is an accountant, and we will be joining forces to do more. So read it and be blessed.

INTRODUCTION

I am indeed thankful for this great and wonderful privilege of producing this work! Many of my friends have encouraged, inspired, and exhorted me to finally produce a work that would help so many people who experience financial difficulty. For so long, so called, consultants, folk who pride themselves in helping folk make financial decisions, financial institutions, such as banks, insurance companies, brokerage houses and the like, have not given the public at large all of the relevant facts regarding the decisions they need to make for their financial future. The information I have learned over the years, the training I have acquired, and the wonderful business of insurance, investments, and asset management, has also contributed to the production of this work. Sometime ago, I was told by one of my instructors in the Department of Business and Finance at Fayetteville State University, that I would never pass the NASD (National Association of Securities Dealers) exam because I did not do well in his business math class. Fortunately for me, I did pass and continued to educate myself on this wonderful industry of financial services, its laws, and vehicles that people like me could use to gain financial independence. I learned further, that much of this information was available to everyone, but a specific group of people were deliberately misinformed, and left uneducated on its availability and necessity. After twenty years in this business, and serving as an insurance broker, agent, regional vice president, and seller of mutual funds, annuities, life and health insurance, I was moved to share with as many folk as I could the simple and rich information that could change the financial future of those who wanted to make that change. The privilege of benefiting from tremendous teaching by leaders in the financial services industry, provoked me to take upon myself the mantle so many have endured. I will tell you the truth about what has taken place in this industry that has contributed a major setback to African Americans financially, by deliberate and deceitful practices. These practices were designed to create poverty that would perpetuate itself yet future. When I learned that Metropolitan Life Insurance

Company (early in history) gave their representatives a rate book for Caucasians and a rate book for African Americans, I was shocked and bewildered. The life insurance rates for Caucasians were 40-60% less, which allowed them to sell increased protection for their client's families significantly. The life insurance rates for African Americans were 40-60% more, which was cost prohibitive and did not allow this group to have adequate protection, because they were sold a different type plan. Simply put that was no accident. I shared with my dad that when he began teaching school in 1953, the year I was born, there were investment vehicles on the market returning 10-13% on investments, for as low as $10 dollars a month. This valuable information was kept from my daddy, intentionally. By the time I graduated from high school, the market returning the same, and the same $10 dollar a month investment, he would have had a good nest egg of over $300,000.00. Imagine if everything and everyone was on the same playing field with the same advantages. The poor do not keep getting poorer; however, they are so far behind, the wealth gap seems impossible to close between the two groups of folk. Insurance agents would come around to the black folk communities selling weekly premium insurance policies for $250, $500, or $1000 in insurance coverage, for pennies a week. They were told there was no other kind of protection for them. Again, can you imagine my daddy, and mother with seven children, with him being the major bread winner, and he dies with $1000 in insurance protection? My mother and all the children would have to go and get a job in order to maintain the same lifestyle. In many instances, the same dollars that was paying for the small policies could have paid for ten times the coverage, but was never offered then!

It is my intent to put in written form a simple and educational model for the average person who desires to become financially free, debt free, and build wealth through principles of money, asset management, finance and investments. When it is all said and done, money is nothing more than a tool; a medium of exchange that affords individuals the privilege of buying goods and services. The more of it one has, the more goods and services a person can buy. We will also share and dispel the myth of erroneous Bible teaching that money is the root of all evil. A second myth of erroneous interpretation is the account in scripture, Matthew 19:16–26, where the rich young ruler confronts Jesus, and asks what the requirements were to inherit eternal life. He was one whose life was built upon his wealth, and was really asking Jesus how much this thing would cost. Jesus answers him, "keep the commandments", to which the young ruler answers, "I have done all this from my youth." Now Jesus really challenges him by saying to him go and sell all you have, and give the proceeds to the poor. At this point, the young man was totally despondent. He was not willing to give up his money and wealth for eternal life. For some years, many have concluded, wrongly I might add, that those who are rich would find it hard to go to heaven, or money and wealth would certainly interfere with a person's desire to gain eternal life.

That is simply not true. There will be millionaires and billionaires in heaven. This is also a clear indication of the misunderstanding and miseducation of money as a tool, how to get it, where to put it, how to use it, and how to gain from it. The following chapters will be an exciting journey for you into the realm of financial independence, debt free living, and wealth building.

I will also explore the dynamics of insurance, investments, and again dispel some of the myths associated with them. When you investigate the annals of the industry of insurance, investments, and banking, it is amazing how individuals have been intentionally misled, and have accepted this intentional hoodwinking as truth and nothing but the truth. One of the largest industries, if not the largest, on earth is there because of greed, misinformation, and the deliberate milking of millions of dollars from the average consumer, along with being the best industry to work for, and having some sincere and honest servants. This misinformation, if presented in the right way and with the intent of helping the consumer, would lead to an economic revolution for the consumer, and the institution would still prosper many times over. What a travesty! To be born poor or to simply live in a condition of poverty is one thing, but to have your impoverished life planned by greed and borderline fraudulent means, when the perpetrators have the same power to turn the financial future of every person around, is the worst kind of economic disparity!

It is interesting that many CEOs of major corporations have used biblical principles, money, and finance to become millionaires and multimillionaires, while many persons who are the benefactors of the biblical narrative live in lack, poverty, and financial disgust. What have they gleaned from the scriptures, specifically the teachings of Jesus regarding money that the average Bible student seems to miss? What principles have the corporate world and some church leaders tapped into, that afforded them this financial free life that many in the church and the world have not learned? The principles work whether you are an agnostic, so called atheist, or born again Christian! Whatever your particular religious belief is or no belief at all, principles are such that given the truth of the principle and the tenet of the same applied, they will work when applied. I was told by a friend of mine to do a serious word study on the biblical narrative (Matthew 2:11–12) where the wise men opened their treasures, and bought gifts to the Christ child. Each of those gifts reveals some amazing things about Jesus' life on earth that are not explicitly stated in the text but are inferred. I am excited about sharing this marvelous revelation with you. In his humanity, Jesus was able to stay on earth thirty-three (33) years, recruit hundreds of disciples, some of whom left their jobs, livelihoods, and families, yet they were all taken care of from the time he called them to service with him until they died! I understand the times were different. I understand the system of trade then was more or less the barter system. I understand that money did not have the same value we may place on it today. However, the point is, the value of the commodities given to Jesus afforded him riches and wealth. These riches and wealth also allowed him to aid those who would walk with him in ministry. Trust me, when you read that chapter, something powerful and awesome inside you will come alive.

Finally I will teach you principles that work regardless of class or ethnicity. Math is a science that has been perfected. These principles work when applied in the proper context. You will have some deep seated beliefs challenged, but investigate it, and open your mind to valid and credible truth! When we are embarking upon truth telling within the context of financial services, wealth, and debt free living, some feathers are going to be ruffled. I promise you the material contained within will be so simple, you can teach it to a four-year-old. I pray that you receive this work in the same spirit I believe I have been led to produce it. I will have *forms you can print or create yourself to help you know where your money comes from and where it goes; example letters to creditors are enclosed; how to budget worksheet; and other tools I have used to improve my financial situation.

CHAPTER 1
A Spiritual Foundation

What has been so astonishing to me is folk are so quick to proclaim, "I have a financial problem or some other definitive problem." The truth of the matter is they really have a spiritual problem. In my studies at Liberty University, I learned we have a responsibility, and must grow in six different areas of life. These areas are socially, educationally, physically, financially, emotionally, and spiritually. It was an acrostic of a hand. Each finger was labeled with one of the areas above, but the base of the hand was labeled spiritual. The point was your spiritual growth and development is foundational and was the most important area of growth. If it was lacking, all the others would suffer dramatically. You know folk who are filthy rich but miserable. Life is not exciting to them although they have the means to buy what they want, and go where they want without any financial difficulty. They are emotionally wrecked and lonely. Purpose seems to escape them, but have plenty money. One of the proverbial sayings of my daddy was, "a fool and his money are soon parted." It is an inference from the scripture where the husbandman is taking off to a far country, and divides his estate to three stewards. One receives five talents, the other two talents, and the last one, one talent. The first two invested their money, and received double to report to the land owner. The last one with the one talent buried his, and gave back to the landowner what he had given him. The landowner not only got what he gave the steward back, but took everything else he owned as well (Matthew 25:14–29). I see so many athletes and professionals who are rich but dumb! They can't read beyond a high school level, but have plenty of money. They are void of understanding, and will meet with folly. If they do not find a place of sound direction and instruction, chances are they will lose the abundance graciously given to them. My point is a spiritual foundation sets the groundwork for growth and success in all areas of life. A spiritual foundation gives you the solid framework to understand the self; who you are, what you are, and your *"raison detre"*, or reason for existing. This foundation ties you to a higher calling of life than mere earthly success, and simple existence. To know God is the beginning of wisdom, and wisdom is the principle thing. Knowledge is great, but without the acquisition of the art of the utilization of that knowledge, wisdom, one is merely an educated fool. Get it, but in all thy getting, get understanding (Proverbs 4:5–7). When you know that the God of all creation has designed a plan for your life that will's success holistically, then you are left with living, discovering, and walking in the path of that plan. It begins, however, with a spiritual connection that is an antivirus against everything contrary to that plan. Why do some folk succeed and others do not? Prior to answering this philosophical treatise, allow me to distinguish between "good success" and "success"! I am making reverence to Joshua 1:1–10. The case for study is the transition from one great Old Testament leader, Moses, to another, Joshua, who has been mentored by Moses all these years. Joshua is having some doubts and mixed emotions about his opportunity to lead a great people, yet he accepts the challenge. Moses deposits into him some principals that guarantee the people 'good Success'! Notice verse 3–5, the historical record of their previous successes, and how it came about. Then the exhortation to be strong and very courageous, verses 6, 7, and 9; as God was with Moses, he will be with us. Notice the latter part of verse 7, take the principle, the word do not turn from it to the right nor to the left, that *thou may prosper whithersoever thou goest!* Now to *prosper* does not only mean to acquire material possessions. In the context of this text, it meant you will *act wisely* everywhere you go. This is clearly a conditional clause. Receive truth, receive the word with understanding. Receive the word as authoritative from God, then you will prosper whithersoever you go! Second principle in verse 8 is make a consistent time to deposit my *word* into you. Keep it in your mouth. Meditate on it day and night. Digest it, understand it, and rely on it, to observe to do according to all that is written therein*: For then thou shalt make thy way prosperous and then thou shalt have good success*! Another conditional clause. In other words, before the *good success*, there is something that comes before it. This is so interesting and fulfilling. It's a plan of action that works! It is not God that's killing, destroying, and stealing your life, it's evil, wickedness, and the culprit of it, satan, the devil (St. John 10:10a). You, too, can be the source of your own downfall. Remember two spiritual principles, "whatsoever ye sow, that shall ye also reap" (Galatians 6:7), and "you will give an account of every word that proceeds out of your mouth." (Matthew 12:36).

This spiritual foundation is like a person who has a choice of building a house on a rock or on sand. Mind you, building your house on a rock is hard, and hard work. Careful attention must be made to fit everything together. Building upon sand is easy, and does not take much effort. However, when the storms come, the rain beats vehemently against the houses. The one on the rock will stand. The one on the sand will surely sink! A spiritual foundation will keep you standing on solid ground. I make this my first chapter because I witness, challenge, try and instruct so many folk in the body of Christ, to know the truth. It is what will *make*, not set you *free*! Truth! Where do I find it? Who do I listen to? Admittedly there are a number of resources on the subject, and many that will challenge you by asking what truth, according to whose truth? That's okay, however, there is a foundational truth that exemplifies itself in practical ways that a fool will not ere! That's my truth; realism, practical application of a given knowledge. The word of God offers you the opportunity, not to become religious, not traditional, but to have an experiential knowledge of what you are doing. Not just theory, conjecture, and opinion, but to have knowledge, but then to gain the most awesome, precious, and powerful ingredient of all, to have the experience that teaches you as you gain knowledge. An experiential walk that there is no fronting takes the distrust away; it takes the big I's and little **You**'s away, and we get down to theological, Christological, and biblical concepts that teach you how to access God! Concepts that teach you how to access his promises for your life! And basically how to *win* in every area of your life!

I can remember a situation that happened to me in the early 80s. I was in a great business, and had folk to see in Fayetteville, North Carolina on this occasion. On my way back home, I became involved in something I should not have, without giving too much detail. I was wrong and knew I was wrong. I heard the voice of the Holy Spirit warning me of impending danger, but I did not listen. When I finally got on the road back to Greensboro, North Carolina, it was around 2:00 AM. The next two hours proved to be eye-opening, enlightening, convicting, and convincing. I got sick as I drove to Greensboro. I mean, I had never felt like that before. I got home around 4:00 AM.

Well I cannot began to tell you how mad my wife was. Can I get a witness? The next morning and every morning for the next two weeks, God woke me at 4:00 AM. He channeled me to Proverbs chapter 7, and had me to read the plight of my predicament. Every morning for two solid weeks at 4:00 AM, the same chapter at the same time. Even today, when God needs my attention to talk to me, and for me to listen to him attentively, yes you guessed it, it is at 4:00 AM. My point is this, you are a trichotomous being, meaning you are made up of body, soul, and spirit. Yes, there are at least two other points of view on this matter, one says you are monochotomous, or made up of one entity, and a dichotomous being, meaning you are made of material (body) and immaterial (soul and spirit). I believe in the trichotomous camp. Most folk spend time nurturing the body, cleaning up the body, improving the body, but do little or nothing to nurture the soul or spirit. In my studies, I was taught that the soul is the seat of your emotions, desires, and will. Those things that get the best of anybody at any point in time, even take control of your life. The body (flesh) keeps us abreast of the earthly. The soul is the only part of a person that Jesus clearly tells us must be saved. The soul, (Hebrew *nephesh,* and Greek *zoe or life).* In Genesis 1, "and God blew into man's nostrils the breath of life (*ruach,* spirit), and man became a living soul." The definition of *Spirit,* is breath, energy, intelligence, and reasoning, quickening or to make alive! You need a spiritual foundation because it is who you are, and who you are is a part of God, your creator! Being disconnected from him is like a child who never knew their daddy; the seed that began your life's existence. How can you survive when you are disconnected from your past, your source? With a spiritual foundation, as you prosper in life, you won't abuse that life, but you will cherish the gracious gift you have been given to live and prosper, and to give back to him who has granted you your abundant living!

CHAPTER 2
Dispelling the Myths

A myth is a tale or fable distinct from a historical or factual truth. There have been numerous ones over the years about this subject of money. Perhaps the more serious ones that lead the pack come from the realm of Christianity. Unbeknown to those who subscribe to the myths about money in scripture, Christians, two-thirds of the parables Jesus taught dealt with money. He had something to say and to tell us about this tool called money. Here are a few myths followed by historical truths of the matter:

A. Money is the root of all evil. Clearly this is not what the scripture says. According to 1 Timothy 6:10, "For the love of money is a root of all kinds of evil" (*The Leadership Bible, New International Version*). It is the love of money, the motive behind having money, and the ends a person is willing to go to, that are not holy or moral to gain money that the text is trying to explain. The greed of the money can push an individual to a place of lawlessness, and inhumane actions to acquire it. Perhaps we would do well to consider that the lack of money is also a root cause of evil.

Rich people cannot be saved, and will not go to heaven. This erroneous concept comes from the misconception taken from the text in Matthew 19 where Jesus has the conversation with the rich young ruler. Someone read in verses 21–25, "Jesus answered, 'if you want to be perfect, go, sell your possessions and give to the poor, and you will have treasure in heaven. Then come follow me.' When the young man heard this, he went away sad, because he had great wealth. Then Jesus said to his disciples, 'I tell you the truth, it is hard for a rich man to enter the kingdom of heaven. Again, I tell you, it is easier for a camel to go through the eye of a needle than for a rich man to enter the kingdom of God.' When the disciples heard this they were greatly astonished and asked, 'Who then can be saved?" *(The Leadership Bible, New International Version)* And came to this conclusion. What a travesty.

To dispel this myth, one must first analyze and dissect the text carefully. Notice that the rich young man had it all, money, youth, power and even good intentions. What has always been available to him, because of his wealth, is now unavailable, and because he has always been able to buy what he wanted, or get what he wanted, it is now denied him so to speak. His heart condition is raging with mixed emotions. He cannot think objectively. He cannot make sound decisions apart from the influence of his wealth. Jesus did not mean that if you are rich or wealthy you cannot be saved or get into heaven. He was pointing out the condition of the heart of the rich young man. He was not willing to give up his earthly riches for eternity since he could not buy it. Perhaps he did not know how to part with it since in his heart it made him who he was. The needle here is twofold. Some theologians believe he is literally referring to a needle (what some sow clothes with), while others believe the needle was a narrow passageway through one of the alleys of the city that a camel could not pass through. Again, Jesus refers to the heart condition when he says it would be easier for a camel to go through that passageway than for a rich person, heart condition, to get into heaven. Another scriptural reference that also sums up this heart condition is Matthew 6:19–21, "Do not store up for yourselves treasures on earth, where moth and rust destroy, and where thieves break in and steal. But store up for yourselves treasures in heaven, where moth and rust do not destroy, and where thieves do not break in and steal. For where your treasure is, there your heart will be also." *(The Leadership Bible, New International Version)*. When a person's possessions possess them so they are blind to truth, or in this young man's case, he was not willing to part with his riches for eternal life, they miss an eternal blessing and destiny.

B. All rich people stole or took the riches from someone else: the parables Jesus taught (Matthew 25:14–30) on money illustrate principles that work, whether one is wealthy or poor, saved or lost (believer or unbeliever). They work for anyone who exercises and put to work the principles of how to gain wealth, how to invest money, and how to produce more. Admittedly, there have been some who exploited the ignorance of others to covet what they had, how unfortunate. There were some who utilized illegal means of acquiring riches, only to die broke or land in jail. The principle applied here is what you sow, you shall reap. On the other hand, some ended up with nothing, because they did not produce more with what they had, while others did not know all the vehicles available to them to produce more. I will discuss this in a later chapter. At any rate, another scripture comes to mind here, and it too is one of the parables on money Jesus taught. In Matthew 25:14–30, three men were given money that did not belong to them, but was entrusted to them. One was given five talents, another was given two talents, and the last man was given one talent (the talent was the Jewish weight and medium of exchange). The first two doubled what was given to them, and returned it back to the owner. The last man hid what he was given, and returned it back to the owner, without producing more. Now something interesting is revealed here. The first two were made rulers over much because of their faithfulness over the little. The last one had all he possessed taken away from him, and given to the first two who produced more. My point here is money in circulation is God in action. I believe opportunity is not based on whether you are black or white, rich or poor, but on taking what you have, and producing more out of it. It is a principle. If you work the principle, it will work for you! Make sure you read chapter 6. There I will expound upon this principle both spiritually and mathematically.

C. Money is wealth: nothing can be further from the truth. Many folk believe that money is wealth, so let's discover the difference. Money is a tool that allows us to buy goods and services. The more money you have, the more goods and services you can buy. Money can make you rich, but not wealthy. Money can lead you to the place of wealth, but is not wealth. Wealth is having money or income producing ventures that pay you even if you do not go to work or even have a job. For example, NBA and professional athletes are possibly rich, but the folk who write their checks are wealthy! Employees who work for a company could possibly be rich, but the CEOs and presidents who pay them are wealthy! That's the difference. Wealth can be acquired through money, but having money does not make one wealthy. Deuteronomy chapter 8:18 reminded the children of Israel that God grants wealth; "I will give thee power to obtain wealth, not money, but wealth" *(The Comparative Bible, King James Version)*. He wanted them to be reminded that God made provision for them, and it is his prerogative to give wealth. Now if God gives one power to obtain wealth, what is it that the Jewish people know that many of us same void of? God certainly is not prejudice! The word clearly tells us "He is no respecter of person" (Romans 2:11).

The next chapter will give greater detail as to this tool called money. These are just a few myths about money. I will dispel more throughout the book. Stay on point!

CHAPTER 3
What is Money?

As noted in the last chapter, money is a medium of exchange all over the world. In most countries, it takes money to buy goods and services. To get to any country in the world, you must travel; in order to travel it takes the purchase of a ticket that cost money. In the days of Jesus, in times earlier as well as sometime after Jesus' day, many used what was known as the barter system. They would trade off goods or services for something of value from the other person. Someone may have a great crop of grapes. Another person may only have their services to pick the grapes. They would simply trade off the value of the service for that value in grapes. Someone would have a great number sheep in need of the services of a ram. No money would exchange hands, just the use of the services of the other animals. In our country, America, money is used as purchasing power. It is a tool. Not a weapon as some may use it. Money has been touted as the only way to purchase goods and services. In the last chapter, one of the myths was money is the root of all evil. We cleared that myth by quoting the scriptural text in its proper context. The love of money is the root of all evil, (1 Timothy 6:10), the evil or wickedness a person is willing to commit in order to have money. The ends a person will go, forfeiting moral, spiritual, and civil laws in order to acquire this tool called money. That text is outlining a love that is not of God, in order to get money. Several years ago, in the '70s, the Ojays had a song that was called "For the Love of Money", and it outlined what folk were willing to do for money. In that same period of time, a well-known preacher, prophet, pastor and teacher, Reverend Ike, posed the premise that "the lack of money is the root of all evil." He also had a very valid point. Although some accused him of twisting the scriptures around, it was a true and relevant fact that many folk, then and today, were willing to do anything to get money because of their lack of money. Money is important, but not at the cost of one's integrity, soul, or life. It is not that important.

This book is designed to teach those who have a lack of knowledge about money, and a lack of knowledge of investing and making money, how to utilize principles taught in scripture and other well-known money tool books to get money, and also to obtain wealth. I believe it is because of an individual's lack of understanding of this tool called money, that many are living in poverty, and beneath a blessed privilege available to them. Folk cannot acquire the money they need because of this misunderstanding, and because of a poor money concept. Couple that with the fact that many are not aware that they will make lots of money in their lifetime. It is not how much you make as it is what you do with what you make. Given the right principles and knowledge of how to apply them, most people can become financially independent. The first principle of understanding money is to understand the principle of financial stewardship. Money is in abundance. The ability to get it, keep it, and make more of it, is the paramount problem. It is also a simple principle. Psalm 24:1, promotes this first principle, "The earth is the Lord's, and all it contains, the world and those who dwell in it." This tool was not necessary at one time, but because of man's intent to control the world and all that is in it along with the desire to edge God out, the creator, of this world and all that it contains, God gave it over to them, through the dispensation of human government. This meant that man would rule over man. With this, came the concept of leveraging power to gain more than the next person. Please do not forget or lose sight of this fact, *money is in abundance*! There is enough in the world that every person would have an income of twenty to twenty-five thousand dollars annually, and no one would be without. An all important factor entered the equation, *greed*, and now the mad dash to get this tool. I want more than you, so I can have more leveraging power than you, while those without or with little keep saying, *Lord if I had more money*. Some of the Christian faith have even left their faith and trust in God to try the lottery, scratch offs, and gambling in order to have a piece of this abundance. Some have resorted to violence, drugs, drug dealing, and other illegal enterprises, to get a piece of this abundance. Everybody wants a piece of this thing called money. It is a tool, a medium of exchange that affords us the purchasing power to buy goods and services throughout the world. The more money we have, the greater the purchasing power.

On the other side of the spectrum, there are those who use money as power; corrupt power and constructive power, controlling power and convenient power. I was talking with my wife as we pondered our ministry and life situation. I made the statement to her that everything we need to do and want to do is hindered by the lack of money. The land we want to purchase for the facility we envision for the ministry has not come to fruition because of money. If we had the cash on hand, we would simply present our debit card or a check. Money gives you leveraging power to do the good things we dream of doing. The scripture clearly brings home this point in Ecclesiastes 10:19, "A feast is made for laughter, and wine maketh merry; but money answereth all things." Money is a tool that gives one power to do good things. Money will change your address, what you drive, what you wear, where you go and how often. Money can change conditions of blight, lack, and poverty when placed in the right hands. It is a tool, nothing more. Again, it is more important what you do with it than how much of it you have. The success a person realizes begins with the right financial principle. Again, that principle begins with God. It is a principle that will free individuals from the bondage of needing more. When you consider how much you have made compared to what you have as evidence of what you have made, it enlightens you to this principle. If a person makes $10,000 a year, for forty years they have earned $400,000 over that period. If you double that income annually, that is earning power over forty years of $800,000. If persons in this example have not understood the financial principle of stewardship, they will always have an attitude of needing more because they have not taken into account what they did with what they earned. Folk also have the wrong concept that the acquisition of things makes one successful. I will discuss this in greater detail in chapter 4. Money is a tool, and how you use the tool will lead you to financial success or disaster. What you understand about your tool will lead you to financial success or disaster. How you apply the principles will either make you the lender or the borrower, the rich or the poor, the entrepreneur or the employee, the owner or the renter! Remember again, the parable Jesus taught in Matthew 25 about the three men who were given the talents. The two who took what they had, and produced more earned the right to have more. The one who did nothing with what he had was stripped of all his assets. In all cases a principle was applied. Knowing the right principle to apply will either afford you more or less than what you began with. Listen, "Wisdom is the principal thing; therefore get wisdom, and with all thy getting get understanding," Proverbs 4:7. When you learn how to apply money principles, you can literally become rich and wealthy. It's too late when you no longer have breath in your body. If you have opportunity and understanding coupled with earning power, you can achieve this dream of financial independence and wealth. Money is a tool; a medium of exchange in this country and all over the world, to buy goods and services. The more of it you have, the more goods and services you can acquire. It is a *tool*. Learn how to use your tool.

CHAPTER 4
Asset Management

In the last chapter, money was defined. At least we can agree that money is a tool used to buy goods and services. Money is also a medium of exchange. The more of it we have, the greater purchasing power we have. We can also agree that what we do with our money is as important, if not more important, as how much of it we have. I have titled this chapter *Asset Management*. How are you doing with managing what you have in your portfolio of assets?

An asset is something owned that gives or creates value. It adds to your personal well-being, wealth, and net worth. A liability takes away from your well-being. An asset can be money, property and income producing property, collectibles, investments, retirement accounts, bank accounts, life insurance policies, and some antiques. The items mentioned above are an asset as long as they produce equity and increasing value, or a future benefit. If they produce a decreasing value, they are a liability. The art of creating wealth depends upon how well you manage your assets, or how well persons hired to manage your assets perform. At any rate, the management, how well you apply financially sound principles, and professional guidance of your assets, is a skill that many folk are void of. Many folk will just put their money in the bank, and let it sit. Some will have valuables that are never insured or registered, and will just exist without any knowledge of their value.

Management of your assets is a long and meticulous process that may take a lifetime. Periodic evaluation and inventory of what you own can be troublesome, but necessary if you are going to achieve a specific financial goal. Speaking of goals, managing your assets must begin with clearly defined goals you want to achieve with doable timelines. For those who are not wealthy, and you have to do the managing yourself, it can be a tedious task. Many wealthy folk are able to pay professional money and asset managers to do this job. Well trained financial planners are professionals who do this kind of work, who understand their services are lifetime for their clients. For those who are on their way to this level, I want to suggest some simple and doable practices that will help the average person manage the assets they have acquired.

One of the first obstacles you have to overcome is to recognize your assets. If you own anything, you have started to acquire assets. One thing I will discuss in the later chapter is the notion of having an estate. So many do not believe they have an estate, and it is a principle that is left to the rich and wealthy. Quite frankly, if you own anything, chances are you have started building an estate. So the same principle applies concerning assets. Now that you have overcome this hurdle, and recognize you have assets, the next step is to access those assets, and what value they may hold now. Let's start with the simplest equation. All you have is income, and have no time to build tangible assets. Even at this level, it has been my experience that folk do not know what that earning power entails, because they do not have a system that analyzes what they earn and what they spend. Remember, you do have assets, even if it is only income. When I suggested to my wife that I wanted her to write down every penny she spent each and every day, every moment of the day, she looked at me as though I had just lost my mind. I explained to her that you have to get a good picture of what you earn, and how you spend it. Take inventory of your spending habits. To her surprise, she found out she had more disposable income than she had previously thought. For example, eating lunch every day can become so habitual that you never take into account what you spend because you think it is so minute. When she analyzed a sandwich, soda, and fries at her favorite restaurant, five days a week added up to a tremendous amount of money in a month and a year, she was amazed. Six dollars ($6) for lunch five days a week for fifty-two weeks is $1,560 annually. Now if she would prepare her own lunch at home and take it to work, she realized she could cut down on that spending habit. Let's say she became thrifty minded, and decided to invest $1500 a year into a good conservative growth mutual fund. This is how it would result over a period of years:

5 yrs.	@8%	$9,595
10 yrs.	@8%	$23,909

The point is you have the money, an asset, but no *accountability* of it. By taking inventory, you begin to build a mindset toward setting financial goals that are achievable by making some adjustments. Whatever your spending habits are, take inventory and accountability of it. Manage that asset to help you acquire more assets. When I was a smoker, it was not hard for me to make a decision to stop smoking. One of the factors was the cost of a pack of cigarettes, and how much that was costing daily, buying two packs. That was when they were $1.50 a pack to $2.50 a pack. Now they are $6–$7 a pack. At two packs a day times 365 days adds up to $4, 400 annually. That's not an asset, but a liability. However, a valuable asset, income, is now turned into a liability. Again the point here is to develop a workable system of accountability even at the level of having income as your only asset. If you can grasp this concept here, you are pretty much on your way. To take this one step further, what if you decided to quit smoking, and use just a portion of that asset say $4,000 annually to acquire an asset that would increase in value, and produce some future benefit. Let's say invest that $4,000 annually into a conservative growth mutual fund at a conservative return of say 7% over a period of years. The result would be:

5 yrs.   @7% $24,794
10 yrs.   @7% $59,978

You just quit smoking and invested a portion of what you spent in cigarettes annually. You will create a nest egg for yourself, and possibly prolong your life in the making. Again the point I am trying to make you aware of is you have an asset, income, if that is the only asset you have. One further example is needed to make this point even more clear. You will make a ton of money in your lifetime. Let's say you make $10,000 a year. In ten years, you have earned $100,000. In twenty years, you have earned $200,000. In forty years, you have earned $400,000. Please don't miss this point; it's not what you make, *it's what you keep*! That's the area I am trying to get you to focus on. You are an asset, the ability to earn income. It is designed to be able to pay for goods and services, but it is also designed to acquire riches and wealth. Perhaps the area most overlooked is it is also designed to invest into the kingdom of God, to expand it, multiply it, and bless that kingdom! Another principle we lifted up earlier is money in circulation is God in action! Some folk hold it in their hand so tight, they cannot release any, and they cannot receive anymore. I'll say more about that principle a little later! That's almost another book by itself. I have invested thousands of dollars for individuals, and they did real good on their investment. There is no return on an investment that is greater than the return you receive for investing in the kingdom of God. I mean investing in good ground! Okay, I almost got off point. I got just a little excited there. Anyway, your greatest asset is the ability to earn money. As stated earlier, how you manage what you earn is the key to financial independence or financial dependence.

Step 1, set financial goals for yourself and your family. Where do you want to be financially in five, ten, twenty years and beyond? How much cash do you want to have on hand at any given point in your future? Do you want to eliminate debt? Debt is a *demon*! Do you want to retire early in life or at sixty-five? The statistics are startling. Most folk who work for thirty to forty years and retire at sixty-five live an average of two years after retirement. I know of stories where some folk never received their first retirement check because they died. Another startling fact is there is a move in Congress to move the retirement age up to seventy. There is a saying, most people do not plan to fail, they fail to plan! Chances are you will live, but if you do and do not have a plan, it's a struggle. Began this step with the attitude I will make the necessary sacrifices to reach my financial goals. Many of our seniors are at Wal-Mart, K-Mart, and other wonderful places working because they have to! Another startling fact is many folk do not have $100 in a savings when they retire after working hard all those years. This is again, a failure to plan. If you are reading this book, you now have the responsibility to prepare yourself from these statistics. Folk are in so much debt because of a lack of planning. They don't have the cash to make purchases, so they get a credit card or a loan to make the purchase. Planning will prevent that. For example, if you needed a washer and dryer at a cost of $2100, save that money over a short period of time and pay cash for it. Folk will not save that much over a short period of time. Instead they will apply for credit to get it, and pay more interest for the credit than what they earn on their savings.

Step 2, began by taking inventory of what you spend, and what you spend your money on. Everyday keep a record of that spending habit. I will have forms I used in the appendix to help you with this. You cannot know where you need to go until you clearly identify where you are. Also, in this step, create an attitude for winning.

Stop declaring easy come easy go, and began an attitude that I want to have something, so I won't have to work all my life. Also, create an attitude that I want to change my family's financial future from this day forward. Remember in a previous chapter, money is a tool. It is far greater to have it work for you than to always have to work for it. I have friends who followed this advice several years ago, and now they have the option of living off the interest earned from their investments. They get up when they want to. When you manage this asset the right way, you will move from an employee to an employer, from a borrower to a lender, and from taking a vacation when someone else allows you to when you want too. It begins with knowing what you are doing with your money you earn now, and how you spend it now.

We have established two steps in your comeback. Step 1 is to set concrete, definable goals, goals that are reachable. Set those goals for a period of years, and do evaluations on how well you did in meeting that goal, or how far you are from reaching that goal, and what happened that caused you not to reach that goal. Prior to the year goals, set short-term goals, and records of success along the way. Something simple like, I stopped eating out every day or every week, and I have recorded the money I am saving. That's an achievable and realistic goal that creates success. Also, reward yourself for reaching the goal you set for a specified time period. At the time of analyzing and reevaluating your goals, you set new ones, more challenging ones. For example, you decide to free up money to channel to more productive areas. You stop drinking to reach that $5000 goal in ninety days. Let's say you only reach $4800. Now what you do is raise that goal by $200. So over the next ninety days, the goal is $5200. The point is you got so close to that thing, that it is worthy of celebration. A milestone you never accomplished before. That is a major success step. Once you have clearly defined reachable goals, your next step was to begin taking inventory of your spending habits. How much do I earn, how much do I spend. Yes that's right, everything you spend, no matter how minute, or insignificant. *Pennies add up to be dollars*! So make an inventory of every penny earned and spent. In about a couple of weeks, you will begin to see a pattern in your spending habits. This is good. You should also begin to see areas of spending habits that can be changed. That's good. Now you are managing your assets. In our case, our asset is income. Now you are working your plan like clockwork. Your notebook or pad is next to you, and every time you spend money you right it down, the date, what you bought, the day you bought it, and what time of day you bought it. Remember, you have learned a few bad habits, and those habits are standing in the way of your financial independence. They became routine to you over the years, but now you are taking inventory of what they are doing to you. Great step!

Your next step, step 3, is to make a list of credit cards, loans, short and long-term, interest rates paid on each of these items; and what the monthly payment is. You should also list the balances on each account. Listen, all these seemingly beneficial items play against you in your quest for financial independence. Have you noticed that credit card companies, banks, and loan companies all vie for your desire to get something fast, and know you will act impatiently to acquire it? They all charge you more interest than they give to you on any kind of savings. Banks pay you the least amount of interest on your savings, but charge you from 18–21% interest on credit cards or loans. At any rate, they pay less on savings than they charge you on convenience buying. That's their way of making money, and making you give your money to them. It's easy to get into them with enticing low get started interest rates. This is a devil or angel that most people do not understand. The devil is the APR or Annual Percentage Rate which most folk don't pay a lot of attention to. They only see what the company states they will charge them in an interest rate. When you couple that with late payment fees, over the limit fees, and annual fees, your interest rate then gets a little higher. Now the next hidden tactic is the people with poor credit ratings get charged even a higher interest rate on loans, credit cards, and mortgages. Are you kidding? You get penalized for having poor credit. How can a person in this position afford higher interest rates if they don't even qualify for certain credit purchases? You can get the credit anyway just pay a higher interest rate for the convenience. Now, I understand the capitalistic system we have in this country and the world, but these companies can still make a sizeable profit if they charged you less interest on credit, and pay you more on your savings and investments. It's not a necessary charge but pure greed. Now if you become impulsive and impatient, you will certainly become prime prey for this hunt! On the other hand, if you start now, taking inventory of how you got into this situation, you can turn it around. That's the good news. There will be a form in the appendixes for this inventory as well. It will ask for your creditor, the interest rate you pay on the loan or credit card, the payment amount, the date due, the balance owed, and if there is a prepayment penalty. The prepayment penalty is important because it will either allow you to prepay on the principle, or pay a penalty if you do prepay. If you can afford to do so and there is no prepayment penalty, you can pay a credit owed off earlier than termed by making a prepayment on the principal each month, or periodically during the term period. So it is important to make this list, and try to get these debts eliminated as quickly as possible. You got this step? Please follow them consistently and with strong resolve. Remember you have a goal of becoming financially independent.

The next step is all so important. Step 4, assess your credit standing. You have a right to receive a free credit report from the three reporting agencies once each year. If you have been denied credit, you have the right to inquire from the credit reporting agencies why, by looking at your credit report. As I write this work, I am waiting for an answer from the FTC Consumer Credit Financial Division on why you receive a different credit report than the creditor you apply for credit. That's right! The report acquired by creditors maybe different than the one you receive. You may not know you may have two different files at one or more of the credit reporting agencies. Another tip you may not know is when you receive credit from a creditor, they continue to pull your credit file which has an adverse effect on your credit score and standing. No one can ask for your credit file without your signed permission. Even when you grant a creditor permission, when there is an inquiry into your credit standing, it has an adverse effect on your credit standing. I do not think this is fair. Do you? Credit can be good, if extremely necessary, but for the most part it is a demon! Something created to make someone else wealthy and rich at your expense. Two things happened in Congress under the last Bush Administration that changed the financial services sector drastically, and hurt the average consumer. First the ERISA Act of 1986 and later was amended allowing corporations and businesses opportunity to tap into or use the retirement plans as leverage and as a vehicle to invest into the marketplace. Prior to this act by a predominately Republican Congress, it was illegal to do so, simply because of what happened when millions of retirees lost their retirement a few years ago. However, those who invested the money, and those who knew of such investment got rich or richer off the deal. Secondly, because of the loopholes of what went on above, mortgage companies, banks, and other loan houses, began making mortgages and loans to folk they knew did not qualify knowing they wouldn't lose if things did as they did, took a turn for the worst in the mortgage arena. Hence when President Obama was elected, it was the only prudent thing he could have done to save what remained of the financial, credit, and housing market. Still those who took part of this practice profited substantially. Here's why. When a bank or mortgage company grants you a mortgage or loan, they cover themselves with insurance in the event of foreclosure or insolvency. Secondly, they sell that mortgage or loan sometimes for nine (9) to ten (10) times the amount you borrowed. This is called leveraging. The risk and advantage is you will pay on it for the entire term, if not someone else will purchase the home. When you calculate the amount of money you will pay over a period of time, financiers and mortgage brokers see the dollars that can be made over that period of time. So by selling it to sometimes the Federal Reserve, they then become the recipients of those funds while the creditor who granted you the credit, still remains the creditor of record. If you and two or three of your friends could finance one house, sell the mortgage for nine times its value, that's making money. Five or six of those every six months, won't be long before you can be financially independent. When you prove to be a good risk, this practice may take place two to three times over the period of the note. If you default on the deal, they are still covered, but you are still responsible for the note. If you do not pay it, it will go on your credit report. For a mortgage, it can remain there for ten years. Now here is another trick of the trade that creditors do, especially if you default. The defaulted note remains on your credit rating from the date of last activity until the ten years have expired. Many creditors keep renewing the last activity date so your credit rating may never change. Isn't that something? A little credit is a good thing. But if you can do without it, you will probably have a better chance of building financial independence. If you do not have credit, you can establish credit by getting such things as a prepaid credit card; having a creditor grant you credit on a short term, and ask them to report it to your credit bureau. I began rebuilding my credit worthiness by asking

Lowes to grant me a small credit limit credit card. I got a washer and dryer, paid it off early, and had Lowes to report it to the credit bureau. It's called creating an alternative credit file. It also works if your credit is not so good. The idea is to have enough cash on hand that you can pay for what you need and want. When you apply for hospitalization or life insurance, your credit standing is requested. The company even goes so far as to ask your neighbors and friends about your lifestyle and habits. They want to make sure that you are a good risk. (By the way insurance companies use the same practice of reducing their risk by selling part of the life insurance you purchased to another insurer called a reinsurer.) You also have the right to block your information from being sold to other creditors or information seekers. That's right; the credit bureau can sell your information. Note: they work for the members of the bureau, normally the credit grantors. In the next chapter, I will go into greater detail on how to acquire a greater credit standing.

You are an asset. Your ability to earn income is an asset in itself. How you manage what you do determines your success or failure at financial independence. I have presented to you four basic steps you need to take to start your journey toward financial independence and well-being. In the next chapter, I will present to you more steps in greater detail on how to accomplish your goals, tools you need in place to reach them, and practical applications to begin. It all starts with the above four steps. When you start this process, you can move into the next steps of progress. You can and will make this happen!

CHAPTER 5
Putting a Plan Together

In this chapter, you will find common sense approaches to reach the goals you set in step 1–step 4. You will also learn other valuable tools and principals that are necessary for your successful step progression to your desired goal. I must also point out to you that as you are learning new and valuable information, I have designed it so that you will apply it in a particular step. If you have not done it, you need to stop and go back, and do step 1–step 4. Small successes will eventually lead up to a large success. It is imperative that you do not take short cuts. This is your financial future and that of your families! Okay. I want to say more about your credit standing or a lack thereof before I move into putting a plan together. I began taking the consumer credit counseling course a few years ago, but did not complete it. The information I learned, however, was priceless. First, you have the right to rebuttal any information you feel is erroneous in your file. You can write up to one hundred (100) words in rebuttal per item reported wrongly. I will have in Appendix 2 a sample letter sent to the credit bureaus. As I alluded to in the previous chapter, with the population in America blooming around 200–300 million people, it is interesting to note that there are also around that same amount of credit files. Now out of the 200–300 million folk in this country, only about half are really at an age they may be able to receive credit. If this is true, that means some folk have more than one credit file per credit bureau. You now must counterattack your file by asking creditors who grant you credit to report your good record to the bureaus. Start out with something small with low payments and balances. Something you can handle easily. Say to them you are trying to rebuild your standing, and want them to report it to the credit bureau. This creates an alternative file for you. By the same token, you are also working on the negative stuff in that file. Letters will be in the appendix to show you how to approach credit bureaus. You will win.

Now the first thing I will begin with in this chapter is how to put a plan together. How do I begin the process? I would suggest you have a Financial Needs Analysis (FNA) done. It is not such a complicated procedure. A financial needs analysis will tell you what kind of financial shape you are in, and what you need to do to change it or improve upon it. A financial planner, insurance agent, or even perhaps your banker can give you some ideas on where to get a form. (I will certainly be more than happy to help you in this area!) A simplified FNA will be in the appendix. I'll begin with personal information such as your name, address, etc., it will ask you for this information on your spouse and any dependent children. It will ask for debts you have, short and long-term. Do you have a mortgage, emergency fund, college fund for your children, and how much is it now, and how much is necessary to meet your goals? Do you have adequate life insurance, an income replacement plan, disability income insurance, and any other insurance? How much money do you want to retire on monthly, and how does that equate in current dollars and future dollars, taking into consideration variables such as interest rates and inflation? All of these questions are asked to help you begin thinking about putting a plan together. Once you give all relevant information, the analysis will then show you what you need to do to meet the desired goals you set from this information. For example, if you make $50,000 annually, and your family depends on this money, how will you replace that income over a period of years so your family can maintain their current standard of living if you die? Let's say they will need it for a period of ten (10) years. That means you will need a vehicle that will produce $500,000 at your death, not taking into consideration any interest rates on the investment of that money. If an interest rate of 10% can be gained yearly on that amount of money, it will provide $50,000 annually. The point is, a financial needs analysis will help you plan effectively for future financial goals. This principle applies regardless of what your financial goals are. The needs analysis can show you realistic projections based on any interest rate. A tool we used was called the DIME theory: D=death, I=income, M=mortgage, E=education. Now unless you have the cash on hand to meet these goals, you will then need to purchase low cost life insurance to create an immediate estate for your family, in the event of death. Every individual should do a financial needs analysis. It is good for your current situation and your desired future situation. (***) (I will have a sample one in the appendix). Remember steps 1–4? Can you see how preparing that information will provide needed information for the needs analysis? Another wonderful aspect about the financial needs analysis is you can have it done on each member of your family, yes even the children. The needs analysis is the first step to generating a systematic and consistent plan of action for your financial success. The *ultimate goal* is to become financially independent. That means you want to acquire enough cash on hand that it will begin working for you. That's right. Wealth building is about having income producing assets that work for you, and provide a steady flow of income whether you go to work or not. Now that's financial freedom. Most folk are going to work for thirty (30) to forty (40) years, and then retire. You can cut that in half if you are willing to make sacrifices, and follow your financial plan. It will not take a long period of time if you get started. Given time and consistency, you can accomplish your desired goal. Time, however, does not wait on anyone. It is imperative to start *now*! The needs analysis will also assess your cash on hand, life insurance policies currently owned and the value of them, both personal and those provided by your employer, and any cash value you may have accrued. This is necessary to ascertain if you are underinsured, and you are getting the most value for the dollars spent on your coverage. I'll cover more in the later chapter about buying life insurance. Get the needs analysis done as soon as possible, so you can see where you are and where you want to be. Make sure you have a person who does this, that will take the time to help you plan adequately. (Note: I will offer this service if you need me to, or at least make suggestions). Make sure your plan is goal oriented. It should not take more than a few days to get this done.

The second thing I would suggest you do at this stage is to have a Will done.

Have a living will, to include advanced directives, and a will for your death, done. You will need an attorney to get this done' however, a tool that is also available is prepaid legal. When you join this organization, one of the benefits immediately is they will give you forms to start the process of a simple will. What will the will do? The will states legally how you want your estate distributed at your death. It takes into consideration, what you own, and who is to receive all or a portion of what you leave at your death. The will avoids probate court, and the expenses associated with it. It avoids family squabbles because it is a legal and binding document. You can make it an incontestable and irrevocable will if you are concerned about the fight to gain what you leave. I would suggest you think about this very carefully, and discuss it with your attorney. You may say, I don't own anything nor do I have an estate. Yes you do. If you do not have a will done, anything you own will be left in your estate at your death, particularly if there is no beneficiary designation. Taxes on the estate are another matter that I will discuss later, however if you are the owner of an insurance policy, the proceeds will go to your estate if there is no beneficiary designee! The house you leave after paid for will go into your estate. The will states how what you own will be distributed at your death. A living will states how you want your assets handled while you are alive, but may be incapacitated in some way. Advanced directive is a living will that tells your doctors and family what you want to happen in the event you are physically or mentally incapacitated. Let's say you are brain dead, or are on life support, and the doctor tells the family you need to be relieved of the machine that's keeping you alive. Some of your family will agree with the doctor's findings, some will disagree. The advance directive is a legal document that will tell the family and the doctor your wishes. Listen, you don't know how much pressure this will take off your family and the medical staff, and your pastor I might add. Get both of these done as soon as you complete your financial needs analysis. These two tools are the first prerequisites in putting your financial plan together. A further note on this subject is it does not matter whether you are single, married, or divorced, this plan is necessary. Also, the later in life you wait, the less time you have to fulfill your goals. I will reiterate this throughout this work, "Most people do not plan to fail, they fail to plan!" Get this done! Remember, an attorney puts together the skeleton for your will, but a professional financial planner or insurance professional will provide the products that fund the will. In a later chapter, I will talk about the difference in vehicles and plans to use for your investments and financial plan. Now that we have accomplished the prerequisites to start the plan, let's now get the products in place to enhance the plan. Life insurance and its necessity is our first tool. Why life insurance? Until you have time to build a cash estate or a substantial wealth base, you will need something to protect your family and your assets in the event of death. That's what life insurance does. I want to say again this, too, is a tool to meet a financial need. Two questions come to mind: how much do I need, and what kind should I buy? First of all what kind should I buy? There are basically only two types of life insurance coverage. The first is term, and the second is whole life. Now let's discover, and dissect these two products to see which one is best for your need. Whole Life is a life insurance product with a cash value element attached to it. Below is a list of names it is called: Universal Life, Life Paid up, Endowment, Single Premium Whole Life. No matter what the name is, the substance of this policy is the same. You have both life insurance and a cash value element. A *note* here is all life insurance is priced to last to age one hundred! At age one hundred, the life insurance policy is supposed to endow and pay you, the insured, if you are fortunate enough to be living. The cash value can be borrowed from the policy at a specified interest rate set by the insurance company. In most cases, if not all, what you do to one part will affect the other. For example, if a person borrows money from the policy cash value and dies, the insurance company will only pay the insured amount minus the outstanding loan amount. So if your policy coverage is $50,000 and you borrow $10,000 from the cash value and die, your family will receive $40,000 dollars. Another facet of this type of policy is the more cash value you have in the policy, the less risk at death the insurance company assumes. In the same example above, you contracted with the insurance company to insure you for $50,000 in the event of your death. Your policy has now accumulated $10,000 in cash value in the policy. If you die, the insurance company pays your beneficiary $50,000 but $10,000 of it came from your cash value. They will not receive the $50,000 plus the $10,000. The more cash value you accumulate in the policy, the less risk the insurance company has over a period of years. Now more sophisticated policies today may advertise that your family receives both at your death, or borrowing the cash value will not affect the insured amount of coverage, but I would check it out real good before I buy into that. Alright, regular whole life insurance is designed to last from the time you purchase it until age one hundred or your death. You will pay a premium on this policy until age one hundred or death. Life paid up is a type of policy that shortens the length of time you pay the premium on the policy. Some are twenty pay life, life paid up at age sixty-five, etc. At any rate, these are more expensive than the straight whole life, so eventually you pay just as much in the short period of time as if you would have to age one hundred. The endowment policy is even more expensive. It promises to pay the insured person if living the insured amount of the policy at a specified age or period. For example, a policy that is an endowment at age twenty, at age twenty whatever the face amount or insured amount, say $25,000, is paid to you if you are living. This type policy has been called an educational plan, retirement plan and some other names I can't call now. At any rate, it is nothing more than insurance with a cash value element. Another facet of these type policies is the interest rate you receive on the cash value compared to the interest rate you are charged if you borrow money from the cash value of the policy. That's a real interesting concept! The more sophisticated type of this policy is the variable whole life and universal life policy. They propose to have your cash build up tied to the market place with no effect on the life insurance. Many of these policies, however, that are tied to the market place must generate enough interest on the cash portion of the policy to pay much if not all of the premium on your policy. Note, it is worthy of deep investigation. I will honestly state here I worked as an insurance broker, agent, registered representative of the National Association of Securities Dealers, series 6 and 63 licensed, and am a bit partial to some of what I am writing. But my partiality result itself in truth, nevertheless, that's the reason I am writing this to educate you on what is available, and what you should not even bother with. For 15 years in this industry, and now being reinstated to this noble profession, I attacked these type policies, and made adjustments to my client's portfolio to insure they received greater benefit for the dollars they spent. I was and still am a professional when it comes to the matters of insurance and investments. I always believed in giving the client all relevant information regarding their purchase, understanding they are intelligent enough to make the right decision. I never gave information based on how much money or commission I would make, but for what was in the best interest of my client. No doubt! You will pay 40%–60% more for these type policies for less benefit. However, I am duty bound to share with you truth on both sides of the equation, then you make your own mind up. I am going to make you aware of some pitfalls you need to avoid if at all possible. It is said that this is the best type policy because the premium does not increase, and the insurance does not change. Let's see. When an insurance company prices an insurance product, three things are figured into its base pricing; profit, expenses, and mortality. Profit is pretty much self-explanatory. Everybody wants to do that! Expenses are a little catchy. The expense is the administrative cost, marketing cost, any cost associated with the companies overhead to produce, and market the product. Mortality is a concept whereby companies know by actual experience how many people are expected to die given a specific age, and the life expectancy of that person at that age. It's not hocus-pocus, but actuarial calculations from the experience of that company's mortality table formula. It works! They must have the reserves on hand registered with the various states the insured person lives, so they can cover that insurance. By the way, in the State of North Carolina and most states, a company exists called the Guaranty Corporation (some states may name it something else). It is their responsibility to police the insurance industry for companies that may not make it. Membership of the Guaranty Corporation is mandatory for all life insurance companies doing business in a particular state. If that insurance company becomes insolvent, the Guaranty Corporation will handle the business affairs of the dissolved insurance company.

The corporation will seek another company to buy out the failing insurance company to service its clients. So you are safe in that matter. Those are the basic expenses. But, with the whole life policy, added expenses increase the cost of the policy, but do not increase the benefit. For example, the cash value in most, if not all, policies will not even accrue before the second or third policy anniversary date, yet fifty-five cents out of each dollar you spend on this type policy goes to fund the cash value, even in year one. That's right. For each dollar you spend on life insurance that has a cash value feature, fifty-five cents is to build that cash value, yet none is available for two to three years. This feature, cash value is a cost and not a benefit. The more cash value you accrue in the policy, the less risk the insurance company has at the insured's death. Remember, the cash value is not paid in addition to the life insurance amount. In most, if not all policies of this type, the cash value actually reduces the risk of the insurance company. Your beneficiary will receive the insured amount of the policy, but some interesting math takes place for this to happen. Remember our previous example? You purchased a $50,000 insurance policy, and you accumulate $5,000 in cash value. If death occurs at this point, your beneficiary will receive $50,000, if no money was borrowed on the policy. However, $5,000 came from your cash value, and the other $45,000 was the insurance company's risk. It's good business, but not a good consumer benefit. Note: the cash value you accumulate will earn about 2–3.5 percent interest, but you will have to pay 5–8 percent on the money you borrow on the policy. A second feature that some companies, mutual companies, offer as a benefit, but is an expense is the so called dividend. A real investment in the marketplace will yield a dividend when money is made, and you eventually will have to pay taxes on that increase. You will never have to pay taxes on the dividends received from a life insurance policy because it is a refund of a premium overcharge, not from any real profit. An expense sold as a benefit. Once again an added cost to your policy premium, which balls down to a benefit to the insurance company, but an expense to the consumer. Now we have, so far, two additional expenses added to the cost of the policy. That increases the cost to the insured, and reduces the risk to the insurance company. You may say that's good business practice, but the insurance company can make a profit without adding additional expense to you! Yes, it can be done. There could possibly be other expenses added to the cost of the policy over the period of the policy, but let's say those are the ones we now see.

The second type of insurance is called term. Term insurance has been labeled as the insurance that runs out. Again all insurance goes to age one hundred. Any shorter period only cost you more in a shorter period of time. Term insurance comes also in all kinds. The kinds of term are annual renewable term, five year, ten year, and twenty year renewable term, and term to age sixty-five, eighty-five, ninety-five, etc. Term insurance will cost you 40%–60% less than the previous type coverage we shared above. Term also does not include cash value. The pricing basis for term is the same for cash value insurance explained above. The cost is based on profit, expense, and mortality. There are no other added expense features. The company will still make a profit selling term insurance, but more of a profit with the first type of insurance policy. You can buy more coverage for less money, and invest the extra savings in a better savings plan or investment. There are two concepts that go with buying term life insurance. The first is, of course, "buy term and invest the difference." The second is known as "the decreasing responsibility theory." Allow me to give you a few examples of the buy term, and invest the difference concept. When I was approached, I possessed a $15,000 whole life cash building policy for my family's future. I would end up paying $56–$60 a month for this coverage. Further investigation through a friend of mine in the business, took the $56–$60, and showed me I could have $45,000 in coverage on me, $15,000 on my wife, $5000 on each of my children, and then still have $30 extra a month to invest into a conservative growth mutual fund that was paying at the time 8% return. Immediately, my situation has changed for me for the better. It was still not enough coverage for my family, but an improvement. I took the dollars I was spending on a product; tripled the coverage on me, coverage on my wife, and my children; plus money left over that I could start an investment. Look what the $30 a month would accumulate to for five, ten, and twenty years at 8%, 10%, and 12%:

	5 years	10 years	20 years
8%	$ 2,219	$ 5,525	$ 17,788
10%	$ 2,342	$ 6,197	$ 22,971
12%	$ 2,475	$ 6,970	$ 29,974

That's spending the same money, but using a different concept, buy term and invest the difference. You will always gain more interest on your separate investment than in a policy with cash value. You will never have to borrow your own money. You will not affect the insurance if you withdraw any funds from the investment. Finally, your beneficiary will receive both the insurance and the money in your investment at your death. No strings attached and no bundling. Does that make sense to you? The second concept is the decreasing responsibility theory. When you are young with children, debts, and other responsibilities, you need as much protection as possible to take care of your family if you die or if another bread winner dies. Unless you have accumulated enough cash to provide that security, you need life insurance. It's smart to buy as much as you can with the least amount of cost, and save the difference you would have paid with other plans into a good investment. Now here is this theory in a practical equation. Let's say you earn $60,000 annually, your wife earns $50,000 annually, you have a $200,000 mortgage, and your debt is now $35,000. Let's also say you want to provide your two children with a college fund of $25,000, each. We will give you age thirty. If you were going to provide this income for your family until age sixty-five, that's thirty-five working years for you and your spouse. We need to make sure that your income is replaced in the event you or your spouse dies; pay off the mortgage, create the college fund for your two children, and pay off any debts. This is how you plan, as if you will die today:

	You	Your Spouse
Income	$600,000 @10% annually	$500,000 @10%
Debts	$35,000	$35,000

	You	Your Spouse
Mortgage	$200,000	$150,000
College	$50,000	$50,000

To maintain the current standard of living for your family, you would need $885,000 in insurance protection; your spouse would need $735,000 in insurance protection. Your children can be added on as a rider for $10,000 each. The question here is what would you rather pay for this valuable protection? I know right off the top of my head that for whole life, cash value life insurance of any type would cost you substantially more than buying term life insurance, at least 30%–50% more. I asked a friend of mine to give me a quote for $1,000,000 of term life insurance coverage at age fifty-nine. To my surprise, it was only $541.00 monthly. This included $250,000 on my wife. A man age thirty purchasing $885,000 of whole life insurance would probably pay that. At any rate, you see how we can come up with a plan of action for protecting your family and yourself right now in the event of death. This plan is in the event of death. You have covered the mortgage, your children's education, replacement income if either spouse dies. These responsibilities decrease as time goes on, and the need for a large amount of life insurance coverage also decreases, but the need for living benefits, cash, increases. So what if you should live and you have no plan. With medical technology being so advanced and folk living longer because of it and other factors, you will probably live a long life. So with the same age factor as above, let's say you and your spouse plan to retire in thirty years. For the sake of the norm, we'll use that example. Now you must figure out how much income would you and your spouse need to live on for the rest of your life after retirement. This calculation requires taking into consideration the inflation rate in future dollars, cost of living, and tax bracket you are in at that time. Note: at age sixty-five or your retirement age, you are eligible for double exemptions if the tax code does not change. Thirty-five years from today, the cost of living will be 3–5 times higher than it is now, conservatively. You decide $5,000 a month for you, and $3,000 a month for your spouse would be sufficient for you at that time. This, of course, is not taking into consideration, social security, and retirement from your job. That would be extra, and you probably will need it. This is how it would look on paper:

    Male Age thirty   Retirement at age sixty-five

    Amount needed to retire on $5,000 monthly or $60,000 annually.

    Here's your plan:

    $2,000 a year @9% interest will yield in thirty-five years $518,879

    $2,000 a year @10% interest will yield in thirty-five years $674,714

Now you have accumulated this nest egg, you can exchange it for an immediate income fund that will yield you the required retirement amount. Isn't that beautiful? For example, the $518,879 you have accumulated can be invested in the income fund at 8%, 9%, or a 10% annual return is approximately $40,000 to $51,000 a year. Also, you can set the monthly or yearly amount you want to receive. You are in control of your portfolio, and not the company. Flexibility!

    Female Age thirty   Retirement at age sixty-five

    Amount needed to retire on $3,000 a month or $36,000 annually.

$1,000 a year @10% interest will yield in thirty-five years $337,357

$1,500 a year @10% interest will yield in thirty-five years $506,035

Now you have accumulated this nest egg you can exchange it for an immediate income fund that will began to generate that monthly income. At any rate, you are in control of your investment portfolio, and you can adjust as time goes on. Now you have a plan of action in the event of death of either spouse, or the children, and how things are to be disposed of at that time. Again as I stated earlier, a will guides this process with the structure, but now you have filled the structure with substantive products. So now you can see that it is really necessary to *plan*! We are not finished yet, however.

Let's assume that you chose the term life insurance plan that will last until age eighty-five. With term, certain benefits are guaranteed in the policy. For example, in keeping with the decreasing responsibility theory, you need a product that will allow you the flexibility to tailor, make your policy to fit your need doing the life of that policy. Term policies clearly cover you with guaranteed renewability, which means you are guaranteed to be able to renew your policy at any point in time without evidence of insurability up to a specified age, set by the company. Let's say, you are thirty, and you buy a policy that is in fifteen year intervals. At the end of the fifteenth year, you can tailor the policy according to your needs at that time, and the insurance company cannot turn you down. Now as in all life insurance either your premium is going to go up, or your coverage is going to come down. Options are what you have in term insurance. If you wanted to renew your policy for another fifteen years for the same amount of coverage, it's yours with an increase in your premium, at that attained age. What is so beautiful about this product is you do not have to wait the entire fifteen years to renew! If you want to renew for another fifteen years, you can keep the same premium, but reduce the coverage amount to meet that premium. You can even convert to a whole life plan if you want to, in some cases. The point here is you are in control, and your agent will evaluate your present condition fifteen years from the last time, to see just what adjustments need to be made, or the company will get in touch with you to ascertain your desire, and all that with guaranteed insurability and renewability. It's a beautiful thing when you are not locked into a situation with no flexibility. A well thought out and planned course of action should have the necessary flexibility for you, the client, to tailor, make your plan, and periodically evaluate it at specific intervals of life.

So let's review. You expounded on steps 1–4 with all the necessary information needed. You begin keeping an accurate record of your spending habits on a daily basis. You are now thinking about financial goals, and how to accomplish them. You will have a financial need analysis prepared, and tailored just for you and your family's situation. Once that is done, then you begin looking for the professional to help you in putting the plan together. If you find a life insurance agent, you may need more than an agent. Seek a certified financial planner, who understands having you as a client for life. They will now show you how to fill your financial need analysis, and plan of action with the products you require. You've started your wills, living, and one in the event of death. You have survey knowledge of life insurance, and how it works. You are now ready to begin the practical process of application. Prior to that though, I need to take you into the world of investments, investment plans, tax plans, and the like. That's in the next chapter. Go for it!

CHAPTER 6
Understanding Investing

So much needs to be learned and taught on this subject matter alone. My intent in this chapter is to give you a basic understanding of investments, investing, and distinguishing between the plan and the vehicle. Much of the confusion about investing centers around the terminology used in the industry that helps sales, but leaves the consumer perplexed about what they need to do and want to do. I will make this subject simple enough that you can make an intelligent decision about investing. It really is not that difficult once you understand the basics. Let's begin.

Let's start with the types of investment vehicles that are available for your investment goals. Investment vehicles are the vehicles that can define the kind of return you will receive on your money, also the kind of risk you are willing to assume. Below is a list of some investment vehicles:

Mutual funds	Gold and Silver	Stocks
Real Estate	Corporate Instruments	Bonds
Certificates of Deposit (CDs)	Mortgage Sale/Resale	Annuities
Credit Life Insurance Products		Bank Savings Accounts
Life Insurance Policy Savings		Credit Unions

The list can go on and on. These are just a few of the well-known investment vehicles available in the marketplace today for your investment needs. Now in order to glean a good and functioning knowledge of these life changing principles, make note of the following. The type of investment plan is largely determined by the type of investor one is.

The investment plan will give you certain tax benefits that may lead to greater growth, but the vehicle carry's the return on that investment. The industry has compounded the confusion by using trade words and semantics that give little clarity to the consumer. These trade words and semantics play on the compulsive emotionalism of the consumer. For example, you may want to start a savings or investment for your child's education. The industry may call it a college fund or educational plan for your child. You just want to save some money for your child's education. You may want to give a gift to someone for some personal achievement. No matter what the goal maybe, you must know the difference between the investment vehicle and the investment plan without the confusion of wording. To make this clarity even greater, let's begin with the basics of investing in anything, and that is what you want to accomplish. Earlier, we elaborated on this principle. But again, the goal is to accumulate cash, have enough money for retirement, create a fund to pay taxes at death, have money for a child's education, create and generate wealth, or produce income over a period of time. The goal will determine the type of investment vehicle you should invest in, as well as in some cases, the investment plan.

Let's look at some types of investment plans:

Individual Retirement Account (IRA)	Roth Individual Retirement Account (RIRA),
401-K,	403-b,
HR-10,	Income Fund,
Growth Funds,	Simplified Retirement Account,
Tax Shelter,	Deferred Compensation Plan,

A self-employed person desires a substantial amount of money and a comfortable monthly income at retirement. This individual will probably want a good tax benefit, both while accumulating the retirement money as well as at retirement. The HR-10 or Keogh plan would be beneficial for this type of investor, for the long-term tax benefits as well as the ability to contribute more to the retirement with tax deferral benefits and compound accumulation. This investor can invest up to 15% or $7,500 of gross income annually on a tax deferral basis. (Tax deferred investing is investing your money, delaying the tax consequences until a later time, at withdrawal, when you could possibly be in a lower tax bracket. Tax sheltered is investing your money with pre-tax dollars which could reduce our tax liability now.) They could also contribute to the IRA (individual retirement plan). The IRA would allow them to contribute up to $6,000 annually or 25% of gross income, and deduct that from current taxes. (At one time an IRA was for individuals who did not have a retirement plan at work. Now most individuals qualify for an IRA, even a nonworking spouse.) So if this investor earned $100,000 annually, they could invest up to $6,000, and have a tax bill on $94,000. Individuals who work in hospitals, public schools and colleges, and some clergy qualify for a tax shelter called a 403-b. This is saving money with pre-tax dollars. Rules are different for the investment plan, so check with your professional advisor. The choice of investment plans is limited by the tax code, but the investment vehicle may not be. This again would depend on the investor's goals. Still this investor would have to choose the investment vehicle to fund this retirement plan. The point here is what you want to accomplish as an investor will determine the type of plan you choose to use to meet that goal. The type of vehicle you choose usually is based on what type of risk you are willing to assume, and the return on that investment. Again another factor contributing to choosing the investment vehicle is the type of investor. Is the investor conservative, aggressive, long-term thinking or short-term thinking? Is the investor a risk taker, or do they want to minimize risk? Does the investor want to maximize growth over a short or long period of time? What is the age of the investor? Is income more important now or later? The FNA determines these factors, and aids in making an intelligent decision. The important thing here is you decide based on factual planning.

As an investor, you need to be aware that at one time there were tax codes in place to protect the investor from fraud, embezzlement, and financial thievery. This act was known as the ERISA Act of 1974. Known as the Employee Retirement Income Security Act, it was to protect employees from pension plan fraud, improprieties, and outlined tax law regarding retirement plans, health plans, and most anything dealing with employee benefits. Employers could not use these funds to invest into unsafe markets, as collateral, nor anything that would jeopardize, or have the appearance of jeopardizing these plans. We are talking about *billions* of dollars here. This plan was amended in

1986. Recently, under the Bush Administration, much of the tax code law regarding these plans was relaxed by bills in Congress, and as a result, we had the collapse of Wall Street recently. Employers were now able to dip into these funds for leverage which ended up in greed, and many pension plans and funds fell, leaving millions of employees without any retirement. Thanks to the overhauling of Wall Street, and the banking and real estate mortgage industry, by President Obama and the early Congress of his presidency, more protections were put back in place for investors and employees of pension plans. But it still was not enough. There are other safeguards that you, the investor, must also know, that as the banks have the FDIC (Federal Deposit Insurance Corporation) for its customers, there is SIPC (Securities Investors Protection Corporation) for investors. SIPC covers the investor for up to $300,000 in cash as well as protections for paper investments. Some losses are covered under these protections. Prior planning can minimize and get away from losses. I do not mean to suggest that a loss is not possible, however, good professional advisors, proper research, and staying on top of your goal helps to reduce that risk. In many cases, when an investor gains on their investment, and later that gain is not as much or there is a negative net gain, it can simply be from the gain and not your principle. Many folk like mutual funds for this reason. A fund would have to lose on 51% of its portfolio, for there to be a negative net on that investment. It's called diversification. Your money is diversified over a number of investments that professional money managers manage daily.

As an investor, don't listen to persons who think they know or who want to know. Advice should come from professionals who are trained, and are knowledgeable about the market, and those who have been successful. Investing should be from a standpoint of growth, and not quick get rich motives. You should be secure enough to endure the sometimes roller-coaster effect of the market place. When choosing an investment, never make a decision to invest in that product because of its current return and performance only. Use that along with its historical record. What has it done over the past five, ten, fifteen, and twenty year returns along with the one year and year to date record? Decide to invest in a product based also on its management history, its objectives, and its overall performance. You should receive a prospectus which should tell you all of these factors. You have the upper hand. The market and brokerage house want your money to invest. Take your time and research. The banker executives, at the end of their day, research the market for sound investments. One factor they use is when the average person on the street hears about a good investment, it is probably too late to invest in it. There are some rules to follow:

1. What are the (big boys), the institutional investors going to do, or what are they saying about the investment?
2. What are the major majority investors doing, or saying about the investment?
3. Are the investments still fairly new, and only the above are talking about it?
4. Is the investment still in a preferred stock status?

If the answer to all of the above and other factors is *yes*, it's favorable to invest, it is a good investment. If any of the above say *no*, or it's not favorable, do not touch it! You always want to get in on an investment of stock when it is new. Preferably a good investment is when you have the opportunity to become a preferred investor. That is, putting your money in preferred stock. When the same stock is heard about on the street by the ordinary investor, it will push your investment to greater gains and returns.

Again, what type of investor are you? What are you looking to gain? Are you an aggressive investor (you want great returns which come with great risk)? Are you a conservative investor (you want minimal risk at good returns)? Are you free to take maximum risk, or little risk? Do you seek long-term growth, income, or short-term growth? Do you feel confident investing in stock with the roller-coaster effect of the market, or would you rather invest in mutual funds that take a broader shared risk perspective? So much of what plan to invest in, and the vehicle used is dependent upon you, the type of investor you are! Your professional planner can assist you with these choices as well. There is just about any type investment out there that will fit your investor type. All the information and steps taken up to this point should tell your professional planner this information, and then present you with suggestive investment plans and vehicles. Just remember we are creating a process, step-by-step, for you to gain financial independence!

The final things I will suggest to you are dividends and capital gains. When your investment earns interest profits, a portion is returned to the investor as dividends. You can have that dividend reinvested to purchase more of your investment, or sent to you as a check. I suggest you reinvest them! If you earn a capital gain, you have made a profit over the principal you invested. Also, you have the option to have it reinvested, or sent to you in a check; reinvest it! It will grow a lot faster. Also remember this concept, which I will say more about in a later chapter, time and consistency is a key concept. Again, depending upon your type of investor, make your investments every month on time, and over time you will see it grow! God bless you.

CHAPTER 7

Compound Interest, the Rule of 72 and Risk

(1) A given sum of money due in different time periods does not have the same values, so a tool is needed in order to make the different values comparable. That tool is *interest!* Interest is the tool that quantifies the opportunity cost incurred by waiting to receive money, or by giving up the opportunity to delay payment. For example, if you deposit $5,000 in a savings account and leave the funds there for one year, you expect to have more than $5,000 in the account at the end of the year. You expect the account to earn interest. The bank pays interest as compensation for that loss of use.

(2) There are two ways of computing interest. Simple interest is computed by applying an interest rate to only the original principal. Compound interest is computed by applying an interest rate to the sum of the original principal, and the interest credited to it in previous periods. Compound interest allows interest earned to be added to the principal balance, and it also earns interest. Interest earning interest is what it is called compounding. When planning for the future of your savings and investments, knowing there is a compounding effect on your future dollars, is exciting and comforting.

Interest can accrue daily, monthly, quarterly, semiannually, or annually. Interest rate is a key factor in determining the growth of your investment and how much. Interest is an interesting concept, and it would be wise to understand it. You will either prosper from it or be a slave to it! What that means is illustrated in the following example: Say you deposit $1,000 in your bank, and it earns 6% simple interest. At the end of that year, your simple interest is accredited to the principal only, and you will have a balance at the end of one year of $1,060. With compound interest, the effect will not be seen until the second year. At the end of the first year, the balance will be the same $1,060. The next year with compound interest, interest is not only accredited to the principal balance, but also to the interest you earned the first year plus the additional amounts deposited. Of all the ways your money can grow, you want the compounding effect. It will have a powerful impact on future value, especially when a high interest rate or a long period of time is involved. Remember, these two factors are significant when finding the investment that allows your money to grow at a rate greater than average, plus the time factor it has to grow. It is a concept we call "Time and Consistency." Given the right amount of time, and the investor consistently deposits in that investment every month, with a high interest rate with a compounding effect, the (FV) future value of money is phenomenal. When compound interest is in effect, the future value (FV) of money moves in the same direction as the number of periods (N) and interest (I) (FV increases as they increase). If you do not possess one, ask your banker or investment guide to obtain a compound interest table for you. Through this book, it will be necessary to learn how to use one, as one will be in the appendix.

Banks understand this concept. They really are the institution that makes the money by other people's money. For example, a bank will pay you on deposits in savings accounts somewhere between 1 and 3 percent interest, yet will charge you 14–20 percent on a credit card. A short-term or long-term CD (certificate of deposit) will earn 3–5 percent return, but you will be charged 8–13 percent on a loan. Interest is the key factor in determining the rate of return on your investment, or on the cost of money when you borrow it. Allow me to illustrate further on this matter. Let's say you go to your local bank, and they interest you in a CD say for a one (1) year period at 5%, and you invest $10,000. Could you calculate the future value (FV) of your money in one year? Now what is interesting is the bank knows that Certificate of Deposits is invested in $100,000 increments in the true market place. That's right! They take your money, tie it up (that's the period of time), lock you in to their interest rate (5%), then find other depositors to do what you did, take that $100,000 to the true marketplace at an interest rate of 10%–12% (that's the interest), for one year (that's the period), now calculate the future value of their transaction. We call this bypassing the middle man! It's the most wonderful thing you ever wanted to see. That's right, you take your money to the same market as the bank, credit union, insurance company, government, etc., and you earn the same rate of return as they do. You can do that! It's your right and obligation. Compound interest takes on a whole new meaning now. When you invest into this market and you profit from your transaction, you earn dividends and capital gains. So the same $10,000 is invested into the market, and now your investment company sends you a letter, and says we have profited from our investment strategies and will pay you a dividend. Again, will you receive the dividend in cash, or will you reinvest the dividend back into your investment? Note: Reinvesting your dividend or capital gain back into your investment will simply cause it to grow greater and faster. It's having money you did not come up with being applied to your investment. You facilitate the option based on your financial objective. *Remember your goal!* You have made a profit over and above the $10,000 you invested, and is entitled to a capital gain. Will you receive the capital gain in cash, or will you reinvest it back into your investment? Can you see the compounding effect by taking the profit and interest you've earned, and reinvest it so it can get the same profit and dividend effect the next time one is declared? At some point in time, I really have to do these calculations, and I am just excited to do them just thinking about the possibility. Wow! Really going to get interesting now. That's why Warren Buffet has capitalized on the stock market when others are fearful of the market. He has become a billionaire by investing in the market place that generates him the greatest return on his investment. Investors like him are consistent in making those investments on a timely basis; they are patient with the time it takes to really gain, and build the wealth they now enjoy, and they look for the investment that generates the best opportunity for their investment to grow safely, at the lowest cost, yet grow large over time. You, too, have the same kind of vehicles available to you as an investor if you would only understand interest, return, time and consistency, patience, and a lack of fear. Well here, we will use the example of that same $1,000 placed in a savings account at your local bank, and placed into a conservative growth mutual fund over the same period of time. We will make an annual deposit of $1,000.

BANK	(6%)	Mutual Fund	(10%)
5 yrs	$6,008.00	5 yrs	$6,817.00
10 yrs	$14,117.00	10 yrs	$18,055.00
20 yrs	$39,838.00	20 yrs	$67,126.00

I remind you once again that we are investing the same $1,000 over the same period of time each year. The difference is gaining more interest that has a compounding effect that also makes the (FV) future value more attractive. Now that's investing for maximum return! It's available to the average consumer as well, and hopefully through this work, you will gain the knowledge and confidence you need to be a successful investor.

When considering an investment, you should compare its performance over a period of time, and not just consider the current interest or rate of return. What this simply means is you have to do some homework. Ask the banker, securities dealer, to see the record of the investment you choose. The bank is simple in that, they just show you their track record over a period of years. I would suggest one year, five years, ten years, and since its inception (when did the investment begin). What has the rate of return been in any one of those periods of time, and has it been consistent. With an investment in the stock or mutual fund market, you need a prospectus. This instrument tells you the management philosophy of the fund manager; the success of the manager over the years, the objective of the fund, the companies that make up the investment portfolio of the fund, and what their rates of return have been over the same period of years, one, five, ten, and since its inception. That gives you a valid track record of how the managers are growing their portfolios in order that the fund or the bank will prosper. A second caution or tip I will share with you is in reference to the pure stock investment, which your investment is deposited in one particular stock. You must have courage and patience with the roller-coaster ride of the market place. There will be gains, and there will be no gains. With stock mutual funds, your investment is diversified within that fund. That means your fund portfolio managers look for the soundest investment companies across the globe, and bring them from different market venues: banking, medicine and health care, technology, minerals, industrialization, etc. The fund now has such a diverse feature that 51% of the companies, or fund, would have to lose in order for your investment to incur a loss! With that diversity feature and fund managers, you will win most of the time. That's why funds are constantly changing companies for investment purposes, and sometimes managers as well. They want to make money, and make money for their investors! There is a simple rule that you can use to also help in making a decision on a particular investment. It is called the Rule of 72! This rule simply states you can take any interest rate and divide it into 72, and it will tell you how long it will take a given amount of money to double. Let's look at a few examples. If you had $10,000 accumulated and you could get a 10% interest rate on that money, it would double every 7.2 years with no additional deposits, and the interest rate remain current. So in 7.2 years, that $10,000 would have turned into $20,000. In another 7.2 years, it would be $40,000. Suppose you could find a good investment averaging 14% return. Your money would double every 5.2 years. With the same $10,000 invested at 14%, it would be $20,000 in 5.2 years. It would grow to $40,000 in another 5.2 years, $80,000 in another 5.2 years. That's without adding the interest accumulation. The lesson here it seems is to find the vehicle that will generate the maximum amount of interest return so your money can grow larger and in a shorter period of time. This is an amazing revelation and a good tool to know when trying to make that decision of a good investment. A great friend of mine use to coin the phrase, "Math is a science that has been perfected." John C. Lennon was imminently correct. This rule is a mathematical fact. Listen, some have said that what you don't know can't hurt you. I beg to differ. As I have always said, you will make a lot of money in your lifetime. What you do or do not do with it centers on what you know or not, and who you know that may know what you need to know to prosper financially.

Finally, it is not so much what you make as it is what you keep. Have you noticed folk who have acquired things, but have little or no real assets, cash or otherwise? By reading this work, you are now a knowledgeable person about principles that will change your financial future and that of your family. Listen, take full advantage of this information, and become a lender and not a borrower! The Rule of 72 is not a new concept, but has been around for centuries. If you have a substantial sum of money in a place that is not giving you the maximum return on your money available, do some research, test the different interest rates, and divide them into 72, and realize what the possibilities can be. If you have a retirement fund you are about to tap into it, think about a rollover into a vehicle that generates a higher rate of interest. An income fund may be an option for you rather than the company retirement payout formula. You want a vehicle that generates a monthly income plus earn interest as you receive that monthly income, and has the possibility of accumulating a greater amount of money in your fund. Now that's exciting!

Let's say a little about *risk*, another concept that many do not understand. I take a risk every time I leave my home each morning. I take a risk to get behind the wheel of my car, and get on one of the roadways. Risk is always present in all walks of life. So when it comes to taking risk in the financial market place, what seems to be the problem? I remember folk questioning an investment Hillary Clinton made of $1,000 and it returned $99,000. Well there are investments out there like that, but are very risky! Everybody is not equipped to take the risk, simply because you could lose all you have in an investment. There are investment opportunities that will yield from 75 to 85 percent return on your investment, but the risk is quite high. Someone who won't lose their mind over a $100,000 loss, will be okay with the risk because they understood it was in the equation. However someone who is betting on the mortgage being paid with the payoff of a great return on that money should be careful about taking that kind of risk. Risk is categorized into ultraconservative, conservative, ultra moderate, moderate, ultra aggressive, and aggressive. The aggressive to ultra aggressive investors are looking for the high return investments with the high return risk. It doesn't matter to them. They go for it, are confident that it will roll in their favor, and are okay with it. Most of the time they win! You have to determine the type of investor you are. If you have not accumulated lots of cash and you are nervous about investing in the market place, you may want to assume little risk, and be conservative in your approach. However, if you can afford to lose or have no fear in taking risk with the cash you have, go for it! You are an aggressive investor. Risk is also minimized when you have professional money managers who spend time, research, and money, looking for ways to make their clients more money. That is there profession and their duty, to find ways to make you money. They are going to make money. So since you and I do not have the time or the expertise to know the market as well as these folk, why not take advantage of their wisdom and guidance, and prosper from it. Listen, banks do it, pensions do it, and corporations do it. They are called institutional investors, and they are taking risk with the money you deposit in them. At the end of each business day, city bank executives run the end of the day's stock market reports, charts, and find the best investments to use your money to make money. Top individual investors, who have become wealthy by investing in the stock market, do it.

You, too, can take advantage of having your money managed by professional money managers in many cases for as little as $25–$50 per month, or a onetime beginning investment of $2,500 or more. You do not have to have literally thousands of dollars, yet. Just began the investment to your financial future. When you deposit money in your bank, you take a risk. I remember learning from my up line manager that if everybody who had money in a savings made a run on those accounts on the same day at the same time, everybody would not get their money. It would not be in the bank as you think and I once thought. As I mentioned in an earlier chapter, you have protections against risk and loss. So risk is a part of living. At least take the opportunity to start out with a minimum risk investment, and gradually move up. I am an aggressive investor. I look for the high return on my investment knowing that it is a high risk. I don't mean any harm, but how many of those reading this work play the lottery, buy scratch offs, and the like? What risks are you taking that you will gain nothing? You are also taking a risk by opening savings accounts that today are yielding less than 1–2 percent interest. Do your research, and begin your investment journey. There is an investment for you. You will find that you are not alone! Once again, do your own research and find a professional who is NASD Securities Licensed, but who also know how to navigate the investment market; someone who either has done so or know the right folk who have been successful in the market place with the right kind of investments. I have to keep emphasizing this over and over again, it depends upon *you,* the investor, and what your goals are for you to accomplish and over what period of time. You are the equation! By the same token, there is a firm, a professional, and an investment made for you. I promise you it will not meet with your expectations allowing your money to stay in insurance policies, bank savings accounts or CD's, and the like. Also, again I can help you, and guide you to the right places. To grow big, you have to do big. To earn a lot of money in the market place, you have to acquire investments that generate compound interest, and build steadily over a period of time. It's not too late for you!

CHAPTER 8
Credit and Debt Elimination

So much is being discussed about this subject matter. It tops the major news stories: The deficit of our country, and the trillions of dollars of debt owed by this great nation; millions, bordering billions of dollars in student loan debt, and of course, credit card debt. We have become a nation of impatient people, seeking material things that have little or no equity value, but places upon everyone a burden to repay. More folk file bankruptcy now than ever before in the history of this nation. Many know they cannot afford the debt they are offered as well as those who offer it. We are in such a hurry to acquire things that we do not think what the consequences would be later on if some catastrophe should occur in our lives that changes our financial condition. As I stated in an earlier chapter, most folk do not want to wait until they have accumulated the cash to pay for some needed furnishings. It is more pleasing to get it now, pay high interest on it, and pay double what it cost than to wait! I learned something about my mortgage when I purchased our home. When I bought it, they outlined what it cost, the interest paid over thirty years, and what I would eventually pay if I paid it for the thirty years. A $260,000 home would end up costing us over $500,000. Here's the catch. The mortgage holder can now go to the Federal Reserve, and borrow the amount I would pay over the thirty years up to nine times that amount. They then sell the mortgage to their counterpart, and they do the same thing. The business community capitalizes, and the average consumer pays. That's why a certain group of politicians remained in a state of anger and downright pissed off at President Obama. He was messing with their money, as my mother would put it. America's consumer who in most instances is the middle class is paying for the wealth of the few. As long as you and I cannot wait to acquire things and the offer to get it now, and pay for it later is on the table, we will have an astronomical amount of debt. Many Americans working for forty or more years do not have $100 in a savings account. We spend to acquire things, but do not save for our future. Imagine if that trend were reversed. Imagine if your savings equaled the debt you have right now, and it was gaining a substantial amount of interest on your money. Where would you be today or five to ten years from now? Your future is coming. Will you spend it paying for what you could not wait to acquire cash to buy? When you are a senior citizen, you need cash for retirement to live on, not the government. They help, but it is not their primary responsibility to take care of us. It's ours. Five percent of the population in this country makes $50,000 a year or more. Only five percent! More and more folk are becoming millionaires and billionaires. Why? They build wealth while others go in debt! (Remember wealth is different than being rich. Wealth is acquiring income producing ventures.) Great capitalism, poor management on the part of the average consumer. How did you get into this mess, and more importantly how do you get out? I can answer that for I was just like you. I had even contacted an attorney to file bankruptcy. I had had enough. Phone ringing every five minutes from creditors and debtors I owed, but couldn't pay them, and they knew that when they granted me the credit! That's what they did not want to hear. I wanted to, but did not have the funds to pay them. Finally bankruptcy looked enticing. For five years, I would pay them, and they would pay my debts. The cost over that period is $176,000. But at the end of it, I would be debt free, accept for my mortgage, student loan, and my credit standing would be once again A+ grade. You may have to go that route. Creditors say they do, but really they do not want to cooperate with you! Debt is big business! What a travesty! I owed IRS $10,000 (that's another book), mortgage $260,000, student loan $65,000. Those three alone took 90% of my income. I've been there. This chapter will teach you some principles I learned when studying for the Licensed Consumer Credit Counseling course, and my experience eliminating debt. Mighty interesting information I pray you will use and get out of debt. My book title again is, "The Believers Guide to Building Wealth." You can do this if you are willing to follow a few principles! I've already given you a few. It's tough, believe me it is, but it is also doable. I'll summary review a few, and move to more for your benefit. I'm praying for you, and believing you will overcome!

First of all, realize and acknowledge that debt is a demon! It is a vehicle for the impulsive and compulsive spender. It is for folk who do not care about the backend circumstances and consequences. They are only looking at right now. I want it right now. Remember the example in an earlier chapter where I said you could save the money you need to make a purchase if you would give yourself time.

Save it and pay cash for your purchase rather than finance it, and pay 15 - 30 percent interest on it. (Interest: you will either be a slave to it or a rich person because of it.) Even the scripture teaches the principle of usury (interest) (Leviticus 25:36; Deuteronomy 23:20; Matthew 25:27). Making a minimum payment will cause you to pay more than double for the merchandise you bought. Now that you have made that acknowledgment. Second, write all your debts down. What your balance is, your monthly payment, and the interest rate you are paying. Third, find out if there is a prepayment penalty for paying on the principle only. Once you have done that, we can now implement a plan. Most folk will say I do not have any extra money to prepay on the principle, but you do. I promise I can analyze your finances, and find $100–$200 a month you are spending without any consciousness of it. That's right! You just have not used a budgeting type system that will tell you your income and expenditures. We spoke of that step early in this work. Here's the plan.

1) Let's create an alternative credit file. Find a company that will let you have minimum credit, and ask them to report it to the credit bureaus. Small amount of money. This will begin to counter the bad (if any) credit. Some will do it.

2) Create cash flow. You do this by using the letter in the appendix to write your creditors and simply say to them, my income status has changed, or your debts have become more than income, and in order to keep making payments, I am asking for an adjustment to lower my monthly payments. Suggest to them what you can pay, somewhere between 30–50 dollars less. The law is in your favor as long as you are making a concerted effort to pay your bill, even if it is only a dollar. Creditors will make you believe they have the authority. No, you do. They want the money, not a court case. Some won't work with you, but most

will. Even so, pay the amount you can afford! This will help you create a cash savings. Note: When you free the money up, do not find something else you can spend that money on!

3) Pay the lowest balance off first. With that increase in cash flow, start making prepayments against the principle, and state it in a letter when you make that payment. Note: You can save up to three months of created cash flow. Start with the lowest balance first.

4) Each time you pay a debt off, take the money you now have available to repeat this process until you now have $500–$1,000 per month to do what?

5) Invest or create income producing ventures (next chapter).
That's right! Many folk will take money they now have available to get right back into debt. Something is always needed. You can now begin to invest that extra money into sound, great return investments. You can also begin a business that will eventually create income for you. Remember *wealth* is having *income* producing ventures that produce *capital* whether you are on the premises or not. This is our goal! Creating wealth. Not just getting rich, but creating wealth! You can take a thirty day vacation or six month vacation, and your businesses are still making money for you!

6) Now that you have eliminated most of your debts, and have made investments, and created income producing properties, you can complete the debt elimination process if any are left. You will probably now be in the American Express, Carte Blanche type credit card bracket where you spend responsibly, and meet the accountability criteria of paying for what you purchase in thirty days.

Can't you envision this? You followed your plan, you made the necessary steps. You were patient, yet you persevered! You gave yourself 5–7 years to accomplish this, and now you are there. The next chapter will deal with creating income producing ventures. That will be interesting. Can you imagine what it would feel like to have all the money you need? You never have to finance anything else again in life! What kind of price are you willing to pay over a 5–7 year period to have that kind of financial freedom? It took you longer than that to create the mess. That's a small sacrifice to make to be totally *financially free*! These principles are age friendly. No matter if you are thirty or sixty years of age, they work. I simply can't stand it to see folk who do not have any other choice, but to work hard in their senior years. That should be a choice on their behalf, not mandatory to survive.

It was fun to be able to go to the loan company, and borrow $2,000 or $3,000 just because I could. I really didn't need the money, but trying to impress folk. You know what I mean. Now for those of you out there playing the game of borrowing money to pay other borrowed money off, you never win at that. I promise you, you are missing something that keeps you digging a deeper and deeper grave; interest, late payment fees, add-ons, and the like. Debt is something you can do without, but you want! I find it interesting that folk will work hard to gain a good credit score, credit standing, but do little to nothing to have good financial stability. Now for the matter at hand. The next chapter deals with the principle of creating additional income through building businesses of your own. You must reduce spending or increase revenue! Learn this principle quick.

CHAPTER 9
Creating Income Producing Ventures

Can someone become wealthy by simply saving money? The answer is yes. Remember that wealth is not becoming rich, but creating income producing ventures; something that continually creates income for you. I worked with a friend some time ago who was a school teacher who asked me if he should quit his job to work with us full time. I said to him no. Save you some money before you do that. The last time I talked to him several years ago, he informed me that he had $40,000 in interest income coming into his home annually. This was back in the late 70s. He had done as I suggested. He saved the money he earned from our business and from other sources, until he created and replaced his income from his full-time job. Yes, you can create wealth by doing that, but it will take a much longer time if you do not make the sacrifice of saving every extra dollar you get. A proven and much more effective way is to go into business of some kind. I know for the average citizen, you are probably thinking, I must invest thousands of dollars to do this. That is not necessarily the case, although having income from something other than a job is a good effort. There are credible money making ventures all over this world. Businesses you can operate from home! Many Fortune 500 companies are now beginning to understand, and involve consumers in their marketing plan and earning income from that involvement, many on a part-time basis. Network marketing organizations are growing by the hundreds and are creating millionaires by the thousands. Note: You must always try and remain focused on your goal! There are more negative folk who are lounge chair advisors that will tell you erroneous information they heard on reality TV or the internet, when in actuality they know nothing at all. They simply want you to stay where they are. One of the great challenges I had was to discipline myself to do what I learned to do on a job. Learning how to keep myself focused on my goal, the number of interviews I had to have to make the money I needed to get to the goal I had set. Day after day, not having the demand of punching a clock or the boss keeping tracks of my start and finish time. This now, I must etch in my mind to do every day to become successful. If you are going to create a business, allow me to share with you a few principles, suggestions, dos and don'ts of this creature. Folk who go into franchising find that profits are void until about the second or third year. On the other hand, franchises such as McDonald's, Wendy's, Burger King, Dunkin Donut, have realized profits within the first year, but your investment will be hundreds of thousands of dollars to millions. If you possess that kind of cash, do your research well. Do due diligence very well so you will realize a profit within six months to a year. You will work hard, but hard work never hurt anyone, it helped everyone. So franchising is certainly an option. As stated above, you can put every dime into mutual funds, stocks and the financial market place until you have earned enough to purchase an income fund that will pay you the interest every month/year, and the principle will continue to grow. That is still an income producing venture, although you will have to deal with the financial markets volatility. At least you are accessing your options.

I usually ask questions pertaining to what will make money now. What can be marketed with minimum investment, little or no overhead, everybody needs or will need, I will make my money immediately, and with only one (1) employee? Now that is an ideal situation. All of the network marketing plans I have gotten involved in met all the criteria above except the one where you are the only employee. They believed in the concept of recruiting others who desire to accomplish similar goals as you, and instead of you doing it all yourself, have ten or a thousand of you doing it. Your income then grows by multiplication rather than addition. Please do not get me wrong. Businesses, such as good, I mean, *good* eating places will draw folk. They will pay for a good meal, and will come back for it time and time again. There is the mortician, who knows folk are going to die. Sooner or later they will, and will need the services of a good funeral parlor! I would say to my brothers when we were thinking this same thing over, people are going to do two things; eat and die! Training for a qualified certificate in the funeral business will take approximately 2–3 years. I use to ride with a good friend of mine as he marketed notoriety items to funeral homes; things such as fans, trinkets, eternal lights, etc. I learned something from him and the funeral directors as we got close. Your first funeral you will make at least a 40%–50% profit, and that is on the low end of things offered. Need I say more? I am simply wetting your appetite for self-employment and entrepreneurship. I have found mine and as I write this work, in process of completing necessary certifications, my goal is to invest every dime I earn from this business venture. By the time I am seventy years of age, I want $500,000 to two million in liquid assets, that creates for me an annual income of $250,000, consistently!

According to one report, the top field for employment and great opportunity for advancement is the medical and health field. At this writing, the major hospital in my area is recognized nationally for being overcrowded in the emergency room constantly! Other than the VA hospital, it is the only one locally. There is such a need for good medical facilities and staff. Financial success is certainly guaranteed if you are in that field. My wonderful daughter is studying for her masters as a PA or some top nurse's position, and she will practically be in a position to write her own opportunity! The field presents so many wonderful opportunities to succeed financially!

Thirdly, I suspect the most important principle I should share with you is to provide a service. Be honest, have integrity and character, and walk humbly before God and people! Serve your clientele. They will remember you, and will talk about you, one way or the other. You have a special something that will help folk if channeled in the right way and at the right time. I usually advise folk that whatever your struggles, trials, and burdens are, they are also your pathway to wealth. You must always remember that when I refer to my former business, it was those folk who came from all walks of life for the most part even business. They had a desire to serve others by helping others. That's where it begins. Now it moves to having a superior product that everybody needs. Those are two key factors in any successful business. Then give yourself time! I have witnessed folk getting involved in my former business, and in three to five years, they were able to resign, retire, have the company buy their share of the business, and walk away as multimillionaires. Three to five years! Now that is exciting to me! That's *real* exciting to me! Most of these folk spend their time now motivating their organization, and going to the mailbox. Did you get any of this? Find your place. Research and know the business for your demographic area. Research and know the services needed in that area. Get your necessary certifications if any are needed. Make the minimum investment. Learn and perfect your business/trade. Make every available hour count. Know how to balance. Learn how to balance personal time, time with family, time with partners, time for training, time with financial advisors, time at corporate events, and time *relaxing* and *dreaming*! Now Begin. Work smart/hard. Write the vision, make it plain! Keep it in front of you daily! Evaluate daily! Did I reach the goal today? What went wrong or right? You have to stay focused. Live, eat, digest what you want to accomplish in the next three to five years of your life, and resolve what kind of price you are willing to pay for that kind of financial freedom. Note: I have found that many folk like to involve friends and family in their dreams and goals. Be careful about that. You want to surround yourself with people with the drive and commitment you have to succeed. Once you reach that goal, reach back and get family and friends. When you make a decision to do something different than you have always done, you must begin to think like you have never thought before. Art Williams use to say to us, you must be lean and mean. Listen, if you always do what you have always done, you will always get what you got! Dare to be different and win! Life is a gift to you from God. You have twenty-four (24) hours in a day just like everybody else. What will you do different over the next three to five years than you did over the last three to five? When you become 100% sick and tired of your condition, you will change it. On the other hand, nothing will happen until you become 100% sick and tired. Notice the topic of this chapter, *create* income producing ventures. You are equipped to do what this chapter suggests. This is an age of consumerism. Folk will buy just about anything. Seriously! Know that folk like me are always in your corner, and ready to help you succeed. We are out here!

CHAPTER 10
Estate Planning and End of Life Care

In an earlier chapter, we begin talking about this important subject known as estate planning. Stated in the chapter was the point that many believe that this is a subject for wealthy folk, billionaires, millionaires, and the like. If you own anything, chances are you will leave an estate to your spouse and family, or the state. When you begin to take inventory of what you own and how much it is worth, it can come up to a substantial sum. Estate planning is being prepared for how the property you own is going to be divided among your family members, and what kind of taxes you need to prepare to pay or have someone to pay when you die, or know the rules of generation to generation skipping. The law has set an amount that it must meet and exceed before you will have to pay state taxes. That amount is $600,000 or more. So when you pass on, if you have property in your name, you own, and it is worth $800,000, you may have to pay estate taxes on that amount, or an amount above the ceiling of $600,000, depending on how you have your financial plan portfolio set, and if any, all or a part are in Qualified Tax Sheltered Plans. When you complete your FNA, it should give you some indication what your future value or dollars may and will look like. I found an example on Nelson Rockefeller. At his death, he would owe the US Treasury ten million dollars. The only way he could meet that tax liability would be to sell off some of the property he owned, or have that much cash or life insurance in place. I mean it had the listings of all the tax consequences, debts, family survival, and the like. But there was still a problem of having to come up with ten million dollars to pay off the tax liability of owning so much. Two ways to accomplish this, a ten million dollar life insurance policy payable to the US Treasury, or sell some of the assets of the Rockefeller Estate. So you have a professional on your team who knows how to set your portfolio in such a way that you handle your obligation to the government and to yourself. There

57

are ways to handle anything properly with the right kind of money managers and professionals who know their business. The point here is when you die and anything is left in your name without regard to joint ownership, or passing it along to the next generation ownership, or there is no definitive guide to pass along your property to anyone else as owner, it belongs to you, in your name, and the tax consequences are yours. I'll say a little about generation to generation skipping, which was a very good technique used by the Rockefellers. What Granddaddy Rockefeller built was transferred to the next Rockefeller to keep the family running smooth; then the next brother or sibling would step in, and assume the family fortune responsibility. With this technique, they were instrumental in transferring much of the assets and property to the next generation, and pay generation skipping tax, or inheritance tax, but not estate tax which could take a substantial amount of the fortune. The point is this, whatever is in your name at your passing points to you as the owner of that asset. If that asset is left to your estate, taxes must be paid on the value of that estate if above the taxable ceiling (your financial planner would know this). Be prepared even if you do not know what that is, or if you do not own anything. My daddy use to always say, it is better to have it and not need it than to need it and not have it! Also, when the banks (which in many cases will shut your accounts down), creditors and debtors you have, learn of your demise, will become vultures and seek payment of what you owe them. (There may be a situation whereby you were not privileged to the transactions that took place prior to your relationship with this spouse. Creditors don't care. You must then request from them documentation such as loan contracts, original historical records of amounts paid, and balances owed, if any. They understand you are grieving, and hopefully you will not do due diligence. Don't send any money until you have all the facts!) If left to your estate, they will sue your estate to reap payment. They do not care what emotional turmoil your family is experiencing. Don't leave that burden on your family. Prior planning prevents poor performance! Also teach and train your spouse, and at least the oldest child to know where those important documents are. Get a file cabinet just to house end of life documents, i.e. life insurance policies, retirement plans, debts, etc. (Included in this book is a guide for end of life planning.) Use it and take the burden away from your family. Life insurance proceeds that usually have a beneficiary designation or retirement plans that allow you to designate who receives the proceeds in the event of your death are not subject to creditor claims. They cannot, according to tax facts on life insurance, claim payment from those proceeds. That is why it is necessary for you to plan, to put things in proper order even after you die, it is valid. A will is a tool that will satisfy, or at least aid in this process. It will keep your family from going to probate court, and having to obtain lawyers who are interested in 33 1/3 percent of your assets, and the system emptying your treasure chest.

If you have not done so, you should go to the funeral home of your choice and make plans for your passing. You can, if you desire, use an assignment from your insurance company to have that amount deducted from your policy for the amount your funeral will cost in future dollars (your insurance representative should be able to accomplish this for you). It is a simple assignment form. If you like plan to be translated and not see death, well it is better to have planned for it and it does not happen, than to have it to happen and you have no plan. Most people do not plan to fail, they fail to plan! There are also vehicles available that will help you plan for this part of life. Tax shelters and other investment vehicles that will give you the tax advantages you need to keep the assets you worked hard to accumulate from being a burden to your family when you pass on. That is not a time to have loved ones make major financial decisions when grief has set in. It's an emotional roller-coaster ride that presents itself as very traumatic. In the addendum, I will produce a process that will make that transition easier for you and your family. Get it done! It is so important to have at least two trusted loved ones to know where all of your important documents are, i.e. life insurance policies, retirement plans, benefits payable to family from your jobs, savings accounts, and investments. They should not have to search and hunt it down. The other alternative is to appoint an administrator over your financial affairs that will make sure all this is done at your passing. It can be an attorney, accountant you trust, and will do the right thing. At any rate, plan now so the transition will be smooth for your family. Again a will can satisfy all of this; however, knowing where the documents are is so crucial. You can have your financial affairs so intact that you know to the penny what your tax consequences will be at your death, how much your funeral final expenses are, and what your family needs to live on for a certain period of years. It all can be arranged in an estate plan and end of life planning package.

There is a concept known as generation to generation skipping. It is used by the wealthy that have been privileged to it. It is a tool in estate planning that allows the assets to be passed on to the next generation with minimal tax consequences. The assets pass to a son, grandson, daughter, granddaughter, or some other relative or vested individual, and then taxes are due based on their liability status, and not the original owner of the assets. Eventually, someone will have to pay taxes on the assets, but that could be sometime if structured right. A tax attorney and tax accountant will know how to structure this tool. It could come in handy.

CHAPTER 11

Acknowledgments and References

I want to take this opportunity to thank and acknowledge a few folk who have made producing this work meaningful. I cannot say enough about the God I serve, who continues to show his mercy and grace toward me daily. I am eternally grateful to God for bestowing upon me this honor and opportunity to write, and hopefully bless others through my writing. Thank you Lord! A family is a blessing from the Lord, and I am blessed to have the one I have. To my darling wife, Shirley, life won't afford me enough time to show you how much I really love you and thank you for loving me, sharing your life with me, and complementing me. Thank you so much. To my three children, Carlos, Mario, and Sabrina, God has smiled on me to see you grown and doing well in life. Know that I am so proud of each of you, and look forward to the day when we can do even more together. My three grandsons are such a blessing. I discovered something so unique, that grandchildren often reflect ancestors of the past. They look like parents and grandparents past during their formative years. I allowed myself to see the closeness of a family that so many families miss. We are eternally connected! God bless you grandsons. My dad continues to be a model for me and my brothers. From 83 to 84 years of age, he had to undergo at least five surgeries and came out of them all like a champion. He is made out of something called toughness that many of us lack. He's a tough man, and I am proud to see him continue with life when he could have easily given up! I thank God for keeping him, and being a continued example for us!

At this writing, my sister still lives with my dad and is a present help for him. Although my concern for her runs deep, I thank God that she is healing and progressing. I would be remissed if I did not thank my brothers for all their love, support, and encouragement. My good friend, Leon A. Cromatie, was very inspirational in pushing me to do and complete this work. He continues to be a good friend and brother, and

I am so thankful for his friendship. We have that kind of relationship whereby we get into some heated theological debates as iron sharpens iron. It is good for me to have them, and I am certain he gleans as well.

Much study and reflection was done to create this work, and I want to reference some of those I have quoted from time to time. Of course, I acknowledge the word of God, the Bible as my main source of reference. I started the Certified Financial Planners course work at North Carolina State University, and some of the information used came from my class work in preparation for the CFP exam at NC State University. Perhaps from my own personal study and the attempt to be good at the profession of a financial planner, contributed more than any other reference source. I had to go back to the days as a representative of the A.L. Williams/Primerica Financial Services company, and my tenure as a representative with Triad Executive Planners because it set the ground work for my experience in this business. The work we did to help folk see the light about life insurance, retirement, and planning for life is beyond reward. It is a fulfillment that goes deep into living life itself. I've met many folk over the years, and some became my clients and as well as my business associates; a well worthwhile experience and journey that has shaped my perspective in many ways in life. It has found a lodging place deep in my heart, and even now I counsel folk on making good choices about financial matters. Get the facts!

Nothing could have fueled my desire to finish this work than the loss of my daughter (Linda) in the ministry's husband! She was so outdone and distraught about his passing, and not being aware of so much he had done prior to there being married. I must say helping her through this hour has been rewarding to me and solidifies my commitment to continue this crusade of proper planning with relevant information for everyone who needs this work. There are those who thrive on folk remaining vulnerable and gullible to misinformation. I have been around the table when family members look at each other, and ask how much can you come up with for _____ funeral? That's sad. Then to add injury to insult, I am asked as the pastor, how much can the church contribute. Yes, in the 21st century. I am disappointed with the unprofessional agent who is concerned in just selling something to get a commission, and the company that encourages such.

I am proud to produce this on behalf of all the representatives who have given their all to help families without regard to commission priority. I applaud you and your company! We have a lot of work remaining while families are still underinsured, but strapped to pay for adequate coverage because of the type of coverage and the lack of the representative's ability to do better. In Forbes Magazine this month, March 2015, there was a graph showing the percentage of wealthy folk (9%), upper middle class, lower middle class, middle class, and poor. What a travesty. Seems like poverty is both planned and a choice; planned by the wealthy by not sharing the wealth building information with those who, if given the same opportunity on a level playing field, would prosper also. It is my sincere desire that this work will at least begin dialogue among those who desire a different financial lifestyle. There is still hope and a chance. Effect a Change!

CHAPTER 12
Appendix

This section is called such because it is apparent to me that many people are lost when a loved one dies, and it becomes necessary to gather all the documents, life insurance policies, and just knowing what to do at this point. I will discuss some lengthy but needed information in this section. You will learn and have a step-by-step procedure to follow when that time comes, and you will know where to find all the information you need. As all the other chapters, I am speaking from experience and the work I've done helping folk at this final hour. You are in a state of grief, and making major decisions is a task and not very wise. It is even a greater task when you don't know where information is, or who to contact with and for pertinent information. So many times I've gone to the hospital with congregants when the doctor tells them we've done all we can. Your loved one is on life support, and the hospital encourages you to take them off. You want to keep them on, and the other siblings say no. You all then turn to the pastor and ask what do we do? The pastor looks at you with a desire to say something, but really has no authority too. Remember this term: *advance directives*. It is a legal document that tells the doctor, hospital, family members, pastor, and all concerned what you want to happen in the event you become incapacitated or mentally unable to make decisions while in the hospital. It will help hospice, your doctor, and your family if that state should occur. Get it done. An attorney can have it done. Perhaps hospice can help you get it done or even the hospital staff can. At any rate you need to get this done as soon as possible. Well now let's say you don't make it. You exchange time for eternity. Now your family must make major decisions while mourning their lost. They are wondering where the life insurance policies

are, if there are any. They need to know if there are bank accounts, investments, retirement matters, outstanding bills, and other business that must be handled, and handled right on your behalf and theirs. This chapter is to help you put your business in order.

STEP 1. We stated earlier that one of the most fundamental documents you must produce is a will. A living will (advanced directives) tells what you want done if you live, and are not able to make rational decisions on your behalf. A regular will, tells how you want your assets distributed, and to whom at your death. It can be a simple will or one that is more complex. At any rate, you need to get this document done. Also as I stated in a previous chapter, when I joined prepaid legal, one of the benefits they provided to me, free of charge, was an application that outlined the structure of a will. You simply fill it out and send it back to them, and they, a law firm (Merritt, Webb), will help you put your will together. Most attorneys can do this for you. Notice again they provide the structure of the will. You will have to use other products to give substance to the will, such as life insurance, savings and investments, instructions, and directions. Beneficiary designations on life insurance policies are a start; however, you may need a more complex and detailed document that a will provides. Get an estate attorney. Trust me, this is where you begin.

STEP 2. Take inventory of all that you own. Get a financial needs analysis (FNA) done. How much cash and savings, investments, retirement accounts, cash value in whole life insurance policies, and where are they held. Write down the name of the company, address of the company, account numbers, policy numbers, etc. Write down all your creditors, account numbers, monthly payments, balances owed, address information and contacts if known. Inquire about if there is credit life insurance on loans (loan will be paid in full in the event of death), mortgage insurance, etc. (Do not call these folk at someone's death and ask them, know in advance!) The FNA is a tool that tells you what condition you are in and the plans you need for now, and in the future pertaining to your financial goals, as well as what financial plans are in place at death. Most agents can get this service done through their company. Get this done!

STEP 3. If the attorneys above are not equipped to handle it, get a good estate planning attorney to help settle the estate of the deceased (anything left in their name will go to their estate, after the first $30,000, presently). When death occurs, creditors will act like vultures to get the money owed to them. Really, they do not care about your grieving. They want the money if no credit life insurance was acquired on any loans. Most folk do not believe they will leave an estate when they die. That's not true. You may not leave a large one, but mostly everyone will leave something behind that they own when they die. It should not be left in your estate, but in a will, no matter how small. A good attorney that does estate planning can project what you may need to protect, that will avoid going to probate court. The rate for probate attorneys is 33 1/3%. Do proper planning so your family will not have to deal with major decisions doing there time of grief. I will say this again, for your information you may be receiving a sizeable estate in the form of assets, life insurance policies, savings, and investments. Proceeds from a life insurance policy are not subject to credit claims. Do not allow creditors to force you or influence you into paying stuff right away. Follow the plan. Have all pertinent information, where family members (at least two trusted ones) know where to readily find it. Where are your documents? Who knows where they are? Who do you have to administrate your estate? Who has the responsibility to inform everyone involved when the reading of the will is going to be done? If the family is not in the right frame of mind to do so, who is designated to make the funeral plans with the funeral officials? As stated above, you should have this done already. Having your documents all in one place, safe and secure place is simple. You can have a safe at home, a safe deposit box at the bank, or a single secure file cabinet, to house these documents. Make sure they are labeled file folders or some type of folder that papers are in alphabetical order, and not just thrown in a box waiting to be sorted out. You can have a trusted attorney or financial planner professional that will provide this service for you as well. The point is get your documents in order and locatable.

As a pastor and trained professional, I have always requested that I will be with my congregants when they have to do this kind of final planning for a loved one. I have seen some taken advantage of, and it's too late after it's done. Get it done now. It all can be revised if life takes a different course. It will relieve so much pressure off your family, the mortician, and the pastor and church.

STEP 4. When your financial plan is complete and you have investments and cash on hand, don't act foolish. If you live or if the funds are left to family, have a plan in place for them so they will not run through the money. Believe me. People act funny when they get a little money, yes, they do it all! A good plan will have steps in the event of death and after death occurs. Remember that document above we called a will? It can be used to create a monthly income for your spouse and other family members, or produce a lump sum, for a certain period or lifetime. A will can control the flow of funds even from the grave. Listen, folk who are not use to handling large sums of money will, in many instances, blow it. I know of several situations of individuals who acquired thousands and millions of dollars. Yet those same folk today are broke! They need money to help them pay $100 a month rent. Help them have something, and keep it by properly planning for them. Some will want to pay off debts which are not so bad, however, it is best to invest in equity than investing in debt. This is what I mean. If you have acquired $100,000, and you have $1,000 a month in debt, invest that $100,000 at a good interest rate say 10%. That's $10,000 for at least a year. It will almost pay the monthly debt. In other words, when you invest in debt, it does not return anything, but to free up monthly outlay. Give your money time to grow, pay a little off at a time rather than all of it. Don't be so quick to buy new cars, and so forth. Let your money grow some more. Does that make sense? It takes time to accumulate, but it will not take any time at all to spend it all. In the book of Joshua (Joshua 1:8), God tells him to read the book, and do not depart from the precepts and principles of it. Observe them and meditate on them day and night, then you will prosper and have good success. The word prosper in the context of this text means to "act wisely." All I am saying is act wisely and prudently. Everybody you know and those who want you to know will have a need you can help them with. When family members get money from you, it is not a loan, it is a gift! The next few pages will contain the letters we suggested you send to (1) creditors to free up cash flow; (2) credit bureaus; debt inventory form; daily spending analysis sheet; simplified FNA; and summary end of life planner.

I. Letter to Creditor: Make sure you have account numbers, etc.

Dear Ma'am or Sir:

My purpose in writing this is to inform you of a change in my financial condition. I have to make an adjustment to the amount of my payment each month. I am barely making ends meet, and I am asking for your consideration and cooperation to keep making payments on my account. I can no longer afford to make the agreed upon payment, however, I can comfortably make $_____ each month until my income has increased. Rather than just stop making any payment at all, I want to continue my obligation. If this is agreeable with your company, please return the postage paid card enclosed with your reply. (See note below or ask for an appointment, refinance)

Thank you in advance for your cooperation in this matter. I desire to continue this business relationship. Respectfully yours,

NOTE: This letter should be sent Return Receipt Requested. Cost more but someone has to sign to receive the letter. You should write or type on the postage paid post card a statement such as: "I agree with your terms above to reduce your payments at this time" and a place at the bottom for their or manager's signature.

Ex: () We approve your request to reduce your payments at $_____;
() We do not approve your request to reduce your payments;

Your signature   Company Representative's signature

II. Letter to Credit Bureaus: Make sure you have social security number, address, etc. They need to know it is you and your file.

To Whom It May Concern:

    My name is _____; my social security number is _____.

I am writing because I have been turned down for credit, and it appears there is some erroneous information in my credit file. I am requesting a copy of my file. You may send it to the above address. According to the Fair Credit Reporting Act, I have the right to view my file when information is erroneous and injurious to my credit standing. I understand this file is free, and should contain my credit score as well.

Could you also forward to me the necessary form or forms I need to rebut a creditor's claim that is fraudulent? Thank you in advance for your cooperation in this matter. I will wait your reply.

Respectfully yours,

NOTE: When you receive the file, go over each item line by line. Make sure your personal information is right. Once you rebuttal any information from a creditor, you can write up to one hundred words stating your disagreement, or special cause for the bad report to be added to your report. Once they receive it, the creditor has thirty days to respond to the claim, if not the credit bureau is supposed to drop that entry. Stay on top of this, and this, too, should be sent, Return Receipt Requested.

III. *Debt Inventory Form*

CREDITOR ACCT # AMOUNT BORROWED IR PAYMENT BALANCE
_____
_____
_____

NOTE: On this form, you may have three sections. The basic format is above. How much you owe, the account number of that account, how much did you borrow, at what interest rate (IR), how much is the monthly payment, and what is the balance owed? List all your current ones first. List all the variable debts in section two. These are the ones that are not the same amount monthly, but current. List the bad debts (if any) in the third section. Same information but for charge offs, bad debts in the credit bureaus and bad for your rating. I promise you, if you do this, you will began to realize you may not be in such bad shape after all.

IV. *Daily Spending Analysis Sheet*

DATE: PURCHASED   AMOUNT   TIPS?
_____
_____

NOTE: On this sheet, and again it will be a full sheet, you write down everything you spend money for on the date, (every day) listed. Do this for a 30–60 day period. It will help you to realize you have enough money to do this, but you are not aware of what you spend and how often. Remember the example: lunch everyday X 5 days at $6.00 is $30 a week X 52 weeks =$1,562.00. List it all, and watch what you will be enlightened about! You and your spouse should do this.

V. Financial Needs Analysis (FNA)

1) Personal information:

                                                          Date of Birth

Name _____, ___/___/_____
Spouse _____, ___/___/_____

Address _____
    City _____, State _____ Zip_____

Contact Information:
Home phone   ( ) ____-_____,
Work   ( ) ____-_____,
Cell   ( ) ____-_____,
Email _____

2) Financial information:

Annual Income $ _____,
Spouse Annual Income $ _____
Other Income $ _____,
Source _____
Checking Acct. { } yes { } no, balance $ _____,
Savings Acct. { } yes { } no balance $ _____;
Investments { } yes { } no, balance $ _____
Retirement Acct [ ] yes [ ] no, balance $ _____, Other $ _____

Indebtedness: Mortgage, Credit Cards, Personal Loans, Auto Loans, Medicals, etc. Total amount of indebtedness. (You can use the form in # III above).

3) Future goals information (desired/required retirement income for life, debt free, final expenses.

Ex: At Retirement, what amount would you need/like to have monthly? You would need to figure out how much cash on hand at future interest rates would produce that amount of retirement for you monthly. $5000 monthly is $60,000 annually. $600,000 at 10% return would produce $60,000 per year. If you and your spouse both desire the same amount, then figures double.

Ex: Pay off all your debts at death; create an income for your family/spouse; make sure the children have educational funds available when entering college; pay off the mortgage; etc. For example, let's say to pay off your debts at death, funeral cost, replace your income for your family at your death, educational fund, and mortgage pay off/if desired. Let's use a figure of $700,000. Unless you have that in cash, life insurance is the next option. We discussed the types in an earlier chapter so review what low cost term insurance would cost, and probably fit your budget better than other types. This is how you come up with a plan, and not wait until things happen then plan. Again, remember, when you are young and have not had time to accumulate a cash estate, protect your family with low cost life insurance. When you are in retirement age, you need cash then and a minimal amount of life insurance. Great tool for planning for now and in the future!

VI. End of Life Care

Why do I need to handle this kind of life event right now? Well it is not a matter of if, but when. End of life comes for all of us, and the saddest scenario is watching folk who have no clue as to what to do when it does happen. Grief has set in, decision-making is hard, and you become vulnerable trying to do such. What does end of life care do for you and your family? End of Life Care is in two parts. 1) If you live and are unable to make decisions for yourself or take care of yourself: 2) When you pass on.

I. Part 1 involves a living will. You are in the hospital, non-responsive and the doctors are asking your family members what to do, and suggesting to them what they should do. You put in place what is called an advanced directive. It is legal and binding on all involved. It tells the doctor what you want to happen in situations where you cannot tell them. It keeps your family from arguing about what they think because it is written out, and gives directions to all of them. Example, the doctor is telling your family you need to be off life support, nothing is functioning without it. Two of the children say yes, and one says no, let's wait. You would have already put in place what you want to happen in that situation. Example, some folk do not want to be resuscitated in the event they code (bought back to life). Well some family members may want to revive you. Your advanced directive will settle the matter, and never be in the hands of the doctor or your family.

II. Part II allows you to have your funeral arrangements already mapped out. How you want to be dressed. In other words you will plan your own funeral. You can contact the funeral home of your choice, pick out the casket, book the cars, etc. You can say who will officiate, and who will eulogize you. Your family will have enough to deal with grieving. Practical decision-making is very difficult at times like these. Everything that can be done prior to this time will be such a tremendous help for everybody. I have seen the kind of attitudes folk have when trying to prepare them for when they pass on. It is disgusting. As a former financial planner, insurance agent, and investment agent, I have seen heads of household take the attitude of not caring about what goes on when they do die. It's sad. Do what a prudent person would and should do. Put the plan in place so it takes some of the pressure off your family.

III. Locating all the necessary paperwork, i.e. bills, insurance policies, and bank accounts.

As stated in previous chapters, prior planning will prevent poor performance. Refer back to those chapters (and the addendum) that explain how you should keep your documents where they can be found. Note: Never pay a creditor claim without verifying the legitimacy of the claim. If you, the descendent, is not aware of a particular debt, it's good practice to send them a letter, return receipt requested, requesting that a copy of the original documents of the transaction be forwarded to you. Do not give in to the pressure!

It is my sincere prayer and desire that this work will position you and your family to obtain the wealth life will afford you if you properly plan. I am so proud to complete this, and help others as I have and will continue to help myself to acquire this goal. We can do a better job at helping others when we have the resources to do so. I know there are those in the body of Christ and elsewhere who really want to see folk achieve the abundance so available in the earth realm. I have labored to give you principles I have learned through trial and error, learned through great mentors, learned through study, and learned from the greatest teacher, our Triune God. May you be as blessed in reading and doing this work as I have been so blessed in preparing it.

COMPOUND INTEREST TABLE
One Dollar Per Annum

The sum to which $1.00 per annum paid at the beginning of each year will increase at Compound Interest, in any number of years indicated, at 4, 5, 6, 7, 8, and 9 per cent per annum.

End of Yr.	4 Per Cent	5 Per Cent	6 Per Cent	7 Per Cent	8 Per Cent	9 Per Cent
1	$ 1.0400	$ 1.0500	$ 1.0600	$ 1.0700	$ 1.0800	$ 1.0900
2	2.1216	2.1525	2.1836	2.2149	2.2464	2.2781
3	3.2465	3.3101	3.3746	3.4399	3.5061	3.5731
4	4.4163	4.5256	4.6371	4.7507	4.8666	4.9847
5	5.6330	5.8019	5.9753	6.1533	6.3359	6.5233
6	6.8983	7.1420	7.3938	7.6540	7.9228	8.2004
7	8.2142	8.5491	8.8975	9.2598	9.6366	10.0285
8	9.5828	10.0266	10.4913	10.9780	11.4876	12.0210
9	11.0061	11.5779	12.1808	12.8164	13.4866	14.1929
10	12.4864	13.2068	13.9716	14.7836	15.6455	16.5603
11	14.0258	14.9171	15.8699	16.8885	17.9771	19.1407
12	15.6268	16.7130	17.8821	19.1406	20.4953	21.9534
13	17.2919	18.5986	20.0151	21.5505	23.2149	25.0192
14	19.0236	20.5786	22.2760	24.1290	26.1521	28.3609
15	20.8245	22.6575	24.6725	26.8881	29.3243	32.0034
16	22.6975	24.8404	27.2129	29.8402	32.7502	35.9737
17	24.6454	27.1324	29.9057	32.9990	36.4502	40.3013
18	26.6712	29.5390	32.7600	36.3790	40.4463	45.0185
19	28.7781	32.0660	35.7856	39.9955	44.7620	50.1601
20	30.9692	34.7193	38.9927	43.8653	49.4229	55.7645
21	33.2480	37.5052	42.3923	48.0057	54.4568	61.8733
22	35.6179	40.4305	45.9958	52.4361	59.8933	68.5319
23	38.0826	43.5020	49.8156	57.1767	65.7648	75.7898
24	40.6459	46.7271	53.8645	62.2490	72.1059	83.7009
25	43.3117	50.1135	58.1564	67.6765	78.9544	92.3240
26	46.0842	53.6691	62.7058	73.4838	86.3508	101.7231
27	48.9676	57.4026	67.5281	79.6977	94.3388	111.9682
28	51.9663	61.3227	72.6398	86.3465	102.9659	123.1354
29	55.0849	65.4388	78.0582	93.4608	112.2832	135.3075
30	58.3283	69.7608	83.8017	101.0730	122.3459	148.5752
31	61.7015	74.2988	89.8898	109.2182	133.2135	163.0370
32	65.2095	79.0638	96.3432	117.9334	144.9506	178.8003
33	68.8572	84.0670	103.1838	127.2588	157.6267	195.9823
34	72.6522	89.3203	110.4348	137.2369	171.3168	214.7108
35	76.5983	94.8363	118.1209	147.9135	186.1021	235.1247
36	80.7022	100.6281	126.2681	159.3374	202.0703	257.3759
37	84.9703	106.7095	134.9042	171.5610	219.3159	281.6298
38	89.4091	113.0950	144.0585	184.6403	237.9412	308.0665
39	94.0255	119.7998	153.7620	198.6351	258.0565	336.8824
40	98.8265	126.8398	164.0477	213.6096	279.7810	368.2919
41	103.8196	134.2318	174.9505	229.6322	303.2435	402.5281
42	109.0124	141.9933	186.5076	246.7765	328.5830	439.8457
43	114.4129	150.1430	198.7580	265.1209	355.9496	480.5218
44	120.0294	158.7002	211.7435	284.7493	385.5058	524.8587
45	125.8706	167.6852	225.5081	305.7518	417.4261	573.1860
46	131.9454	177.1194	240.0986	328.2244	451.9002	625.8628
47	138.2632	187.0254	255.5645	352.2701	489.1322	683.2804
48	144.8337	197.4267	271.9584	377.9990	529.3427	745.8656
49	151.6671	208.3480	289.3359	405.5289	572.7702	814.0836
50	158.7738	219.8154	307.7561	434.9860	619.6718	888.4411

OLD SECURITY LIFE INSURANCE COMPANY
3430 BROADWAY, KANSAS CITY, MO. 64141

COMPOUND INTEREST TABLE
One Dollar Per Annum

The sum to which $1.00 per annum paid at the beginning of each year will increase at Compound Interest, in any number of years indicated, at 10, 11, 12, 13, 14, and 15 per cent per annum.

End of Yr.	10 Per Cent	11 Per Cent	12 Per Cent	13 Per Cent	14 Per Cent	15 Per Cent
1	$ 1.1000	$ 1.1100	$ 1.1200	$ 1.1300	$ 1.1400	$ 1.1500
2	2.3100	2.3421	2.3744	2.4070	2.4396	2.4725
3	3.6410	3.7097	3.7793	3.8498	3.9211	3.9934
4	5.1051	5.2276	5.3528	5.4803	5.6101	5.7424
5	6.7156	6.9129	7.1152	7.3227	7.5355	7.7537
6	8.4872	8.7833	9.0890	9.4047	9.7305	10.0668
7	10.4359	10.8594	11.2997	11.7573	12.2328	12.7268
8	12.5795	13.1640	13.7757	14.4157	15.0853	15.7858
9	14.9374	15.7220	16.5487	17.4197	18.3373	19.3037
10	17.5312	18.5614	19.6546	20.8143	22.0445	23.3493
11	20.3843	21.7132	23.1331	24.6502	26.2707	28.0017
12	23.5227	25.2116	27.0291	28.9847	31.0887	33.3519
13	26.9750	29.0948	31.3926	33.8827	36.5811	39.5047
14	30.7725	33.4054	36.2797	39.4175	42.8424	46.5804
15	34.9497	38.1899	41.7533	45.6717	49.9804	54.7175
16	39.5447	43.5008	47.8837	52.7391	58.1176	64.0751
17	44.5992	49.3959	54.7497	60.7251	67.3941	74.8364
18	50.1591	55.9395	62.4397	69.7494	77.9692	87.2118
19	56.2750	63.2028	71.0524	79.9468	90.0249	101.4436
20	63.0025	71.2651	80.6987	91.4699	103.7684	117.8101
21	70.4027	80.2143	91.5026	104.4910	119.4360	136.6316
22	78.5430	90.1479	103.6029	119.2048	137.2970	158.2764
23	87.4973	101.1742	117.1552	135.8315	157.6586	183.1678
24	97.3471	113.4133	132.3339	154.6196	180.8708	211.7930
25	108.1818	126.9988	149.3339	175.8501	207.3327	244.7120
26	120.0999	142.0786	168.3740	199.8406	237.4993	282.5688
27	133.2099	158.8173	189.6989	224.9999	271.8892	326.1041
28	147.6309	177.3972	213.5828	257.5834	311.0937	376.1697
29	163.4940	198.0209	240.3327	292.1992	355.7868	433.7451
30	180.9434	220.9132	270.2926	331.3151	406.7370	499.9569
31	200.1379	246.3236	303.8477	375.5161	464.8202	575.1755
32	221.2518	274.5292	341.4294	425.4632	531.0350	661.6655
33	244.4770	305.8374	383.5210	481.9034	605.5199	761.3654
34	270.0244	340.5896	430.6635	545.6808	692.5727	880.1702
35	298.1268	379.1544	483.4631	617.7491	790.6729	1013.3757
36	329.0395	421.9825	542.5987	699.1867	902.5071	1166.4975
37	363.0434	469.5106	608.8303	791.2110	1029.9984	1342.6222
38	400.4478	522.2667	683.0102	895.1984	1175.3378	1545.1655
39	441.5926	580.8261	766.0914	1012.7043	1341.0251	1778.0903
40	486.8518	645.8269	859.1424	1145.4858	1529.9086	2045.9538
41	536.6370	717.9779	963.3595	1295.5289	1745.2358	2353.9969
42	591.4007	798.0655	1080.0826	1465.0777	1990.7088	2708.2465
43	651.6408	886.8627	1210.8125	1656.6678	2270.5487	3115.6334
44	717.9048	985.6384	1357.2300	1873.1846	2589.5647	3584.1285
45	790.7953	1095.1688	1521.2176	2117.8060	2953.2433	4122.8977
46	870.9748	1216.7474	1704.8838	2394.2508	3367.5383	4742.4834
47	959.1723	1351.5998	1910.5898	2706.6334	3840.4753	5455.0047
48	1056.1896	1501.4985	2140.9806	3058.6258	4379.2819	6274.4055
49	1162.9085	1667.7712	2399.0182	3456.5071	4993.5223	7216.7163
50	1280.2994	1852.3360	2688.0204	3909.2430	5693.7543	8300.3737

OLD SECURITY LIFE INSURANCE COMPANY
3430 BROADWAY, KANSAS CITY, MO. 64141

COMPOUND INTEREST TABLE

One Dollar Principal

The sum to which $1.00 Principal will increase at Compound Interest, in any number of years indicated, at 4, 5, 6, 7, 8, and 9 per cent per annum.

End of Yr.	4 Per Cent	5 Per Cent	6 Per Cent	7 Per Cent	8 Per Cent	9 Per Cent
1	$1.0400	$1.0500	$1.0600	$1.0700	$1.0800	$1.0900
2	1.0816	1.1025	1.1236	1.1449	1.1664	1.1881
3	1.1249	1.1576	1.1910	1.2250	1.2597	1.2950
4	1.1699	1.2155	1.2625	1.3108	1.3605	1.4116
5	1.2167	1.2763	1.3382	1.4026	1.4693	1.5386
6	1.2653	1.3401	1.4185	1.5007	1.5869	1.6771
7	1.3159	1.4071	1.5036	1.6058	1.7138	1.8280
8	1.3686	1.4775	1.5938	1.7182	1.8509	1.9926
9	1.4233	1.5513	1.6895	1.8385	1.9990	2.1719
10	1.4802	1.6289	1.7908	1.9672	2.1589	2.3674
11	1.5395	1.7103	1.8983	2.1049	2.3316	2.5804
12	1.6010	1.7959	2.0122	2.2522	2.5182	2.8127
13	1.6651	1.8856	2.1329	2.4098	2.7196	3.0658
14	1.7317	1.9799	2.2609	2.5785	2.9372	3.3417
15	1.8009	2.0789	2.3966	2.7590	3.1722	3.6425
16	1.8730	2.1829	2.5404	2.9522	3.4259	3.9703
17	1.9479	2.2920	2.6928	3.1588	3.7000	4.3276
18	2.0258	2.4066	2.8543	3.3799	3.9960	4.7171
19	2.1068	2.5270	3.0256	3.6165	4.3157	5.1417
20	2.1911	2.6533	3.2071	3.8697	4.6610	5.6044
21	2.2788	2.7860	3.3996	4.1406	5.0338	6.1088
22	2.3699	2.9253	3.6035	4.4304	5.4365	6.6586
23	2.4647	3.0715	3.8197	4.7405	5.8715	7.2579
24	2.5633	3.2251	4.0489	5.0724	6.3412	7.9111
25	2.6658	3.3864	4.2919	5.4274	6.8485	8.6231
26	2.7725	3.5557	4.5494	5.8074	7.3964	9.3992
27	2.8834	3.7335	4.8223	6.2139	7.9881	10.2451
28	2.9987	3.9201	5.1117	6.6488	8.6271	11.1671
29	3.1187	4.1161	5.4184	7.1143	9.3173	12.1722
30	3.2434	4.3219	5.7435	7.6123	10.0627	13.2677
31	3.3731	4.5380	6.0881	8.1451	10.8677	14.4618
32	3.5081	4.7649	6.4534	8.7153	11.7371	15.7633
33	3.6484	5.0032	6.8406	9.3253	12.6760	17.1820
34	3.7943	5.2533	7.2510	9.9781	13.6901	18.7284
35	3.9461	5.5160	7.6861	10.6766	14.7853	20.4140
36	4.1039	5.7918	8.1473	11.4239	15.9682	22.2512
37	4.2681	6.0814	8.6361	12.2236	17.2456	24.2538
38	4.4388	6.3855	9.1543	13.0793	18.6253	26.4367
39	4.6164	6.7048	9.7035	13.9948	20.1153	28.8160
40	4.8010	7.0400	10.2857	14.9745	21.7245	31.4094
41	4.9931	7.3920	10.9029	16.0227	23.4625	34.2363
42	5.1928	7.7616	11.5570	17.1443	25.3395	37.3175
43	5.4005	8.1497	12.2505	18.3444	27.3666	40.6761
44	5.6165	8.5572	12.9855	19.6285	29.5560	44.3370
45	5.8412	8.9850	13.7646	21.0025	31.9204	48.3271
46	6.0748	9.4343	14.5905	22.4726	34.4741	52.6767
47	6.3178	9.9060	15.4659	24.0457	37.2320	57.4176
48	6.5705	10.4013	16.3939	25.7289	40.2106	62.5852
49	6.8333	10.9213	17.3775	27.5299	43.4274	68.2179
50	7.1067	11.4674	18.4202	29.4570	46.9016	74.3575

OLD SECURITY LIFE INSURANCE COMPANY
3480 BROADWAY, KANSAS CITY, MO. 64141

COMPOUND INTEREST TABLE

One Dollar Principal

The sum to which $1.00 Principal will increase at Compound Interest, in any number of years indicated, at 10, 11, 12, 13, 14, and 15 percent per annum.

End of Yr.	10 Per Cent	11 Per Cent	12 Per Cent	13 Per Cent	14 Per Cent	15 Per Cent
1	$1.1000	$1.1100	$1.1200	$1.1300	$1.1400	$1.1500
2	1.2100	1.2321	1.2544	1.2769	1.2996	1.3225
3	1.3310	1.3676	1.4049	1.4429	1.4815	1.5209
4	1.4641	1.5181	1.5735	1.6305	1.6890	1.7490
5	1.6105	1.6851	1.7623	1.8424	1.9254	2.0114
6	1.7716	1.8704	1.9738	2.0820	2.1950	2.3131
7	1.9487	2.0762	2.2107	2.3526	2.5023	2.6600
8	2.1436	2.3045	2.4760	2.6584	2.8526	3.0590
9	2.3579	2.5580	2.7731	3.0040	3.2519	3.5179
10	2.5937	2.8394	3.1058	3.3946	3.7072	4.0456
11	2.8531	3.1518	3.4785	3.8359	4.2262	4.6524
12	3.1384	3.4985	3.8960	4.3345	4.8179	5.3503
13	3.4523	3.8833	4.3635	4.8980	5.4924	6.1528
14	3.7975	4.3104	4.8871	5.5348	6.2613	7.0757
15	4.1772	4.7846	5.4736	6.2543	7.1379	8.1371
16	4.5950	5.3109	6.1304	7.0673	8.1372	9.3576
17	5.0545	5.8951	6.8660	7.9861	9.2765	10.7613
18	5.5599	6.5436	7.6900	9.0243	10.5752	12.3755
19	6.1159	7.2633	8.6128	10.1974	12.0557	14.2318
20	6.7275	8.0623	9.6463	11.5231	13.7435	16.3665
21	7.4002	8.9492	10.8038	13.0211	15.6676	18.8215
22	8.1403	9.9336	12.1003	14.7138	17.8610	21.6447
23	8.9543	11.0236	13.5523	16.6266	20.3616	24.8915
24	9.8497	12.2392	15.1786	18.7881	23.2122	28.6252
25	10.8347	13.5855	17.0001	21.2305	26.4619	32.9190
26	11.9182	15.0799	19.0401	23.9905	30.1666	37.8568
27	13.1100	16.7386	21.3249	27.1093	34.3899	43.5353
28	14.4210	18.5799	23.8839	30.6335	39.2045	50.0656
29	15.8631	20.6237	26.7499	34.6158	44.6931	57.5755
30	17.4494	22.8923	29.9599	39.1159	50.9502	66.2118
31	19.1943	25.4104	33.5551	44.2010	58.0832	76.1435
32	21.1138	28.2056	37.5817	49.9471	66.2148	87.5651
33	23.2252	31.3082	42.0915	56.4402	75.4849	100.6998
34	25.5477	34.7521	47.1425	63.7774	86.0528	115.8048
35	28.1024	38.5749	52.7996	72.0685	98.1002	133.1755
36	30.9127	42.8181	59.1356	81.4374	111.8342	153.1519
37	34.0039	47.5281	66.2318	92.0243	127.4910	176.1246
38	37.4043	52.7562	74.1797	103.9874	145.3397	202.5433
39	41.1448	58.5582	83.0812	117.5058	165.6873	232.9248
40	45.2593	65.0009	93.0510	132.7816	188.8835	267.8635
41	49.7852	72.1510	104.2171	150.0432	215.3272	308.0431
42	54.7637	80.0876	116.7231	169.5488	245.4730	354.2495
43	60.2401	88.8972	130.7299	191.5901	279.8392	407.3870
44	66.2641	98.6759	146.4175	216.4968	319.0167	468.4950
45	72.8905	109.5302	163.9876	244.6414	363.6791	538.7693
46	80.1795	121.5786	183.6661	276.4448	414.5941	619.5847
47	88.1975	134.9522	205.7061	312.3526	472.6372	712.5224
48	97.0172	149.7970	230.3908	352.9923	538.8065	819.4007
49	106.7190	166.2746	258.0377	398.8813	614.2395	942.3108
50	117.3909	184.5648	289.0021	450.7359	700.2330	1083.6574

OLD SECURITY LIFE INSURANCE COMPANY
3480 BROADWAY, KANSAS CITY, MO. 64141